Freedom, Order, and the University

Freedom, Order, and the University

Edited by James R. Wilburn

PEPPERDINE UNIVERSITY PRESS
Malibu, California

Library of Congress Cataloging in Publication Data
Main entry under title:
Freedom, order, and the university.
  Contents: The indivisibility of freedom / James R. Wilburn —Why democratic technocrats need the liberal arts / Stephen J. Tonsor — General education in a free society / Sidney Hook — [etc.]
  1. Education, Higher—Aims and objectives—Addresses, essays, lectures. 2. Liberty—Addresses, essays, lectures. I. Wilburn, James R., 1932—
LB2325.F73   378'.01   82-5274
ISBN 0-932612-12-1   AACR2

Contents

PREFACE

America, as other civilizations, has lived through several watershed experiences. Like the rebirth of appreciation for individual freedom which is currently sweeping through our nation, critical events supercede party loyalties and touch some essential chord in the heart of our people.

Such national adjustments are seldom spontaneous. Before the popular mind becomes aware of a shift in direction at the national level, writers, teachers, and other intellectual leaders have often been at work for decades, sowing the seeds of the new ideas.

When a new legislative initiative or a change in the ideological make-up of a federal administration emerges, its origins may be traced to the lecture notes of some humble teacher, planting an idea thirty years ago in the mind of a young man or woman somewhere in our nation's heartland. The influence is nurtured by the writings of respected intellectual leaders, toiling long in the night.

In some ways, this volume focuses on a significant event in the intellectual development of our time. Its essays were written by some of the scholars whose influence has now come to be recognized for its monumental contribution to the renaissance of freedom which has come in this last quarter of the twentieth century.

The love of freedom is a powerful motivator. It is a dependable canon for measuring our efforts in every field, from the White House to the classroom. These writers, from fields as varied as history, sociology, physics, law, economics, theology, philosophy and literature, represent a growing group of intellectuals who are skeptical of government intervention. Some have written from that perspective for many years. Others have arrived there more recently, in response to the failures of centralized social programs. They have come to realize that we cannot deprive human beings of the freedom to make economic decisions without jeopardizing every other human freedom at the same time. That is the theme of this book.

Although these writers are a minority, their impact is far larger than their numbers. Their ideas, expressed with a freshness and energy which is contagious, are spreading rapidly.

Perhaps one of the indications that this shift in American thought has profound depth is the fact that a major institution like Pepperdine University would assemble such an impressive group of scholars. Even more significant is the fact that the scholars would spend several intensive days with the entire faculty of the University, searching for the important themes which, in each discipline, grow from freedom's roots and make the entire endeavor of higher education a worthy undertaking. Such an event is virtually unheard of among American universities.

The faculty conference was made possible by generous grants from the Fluor Corporation, the W. M. Keck Foundation, the Marguerite Eyer Wilbur Foundation, and the Pepperdine Center for American Private Enterprise. Publication of the addresses has been made possible by the Scaife Family Charitable Trusts.

I am especially indebted to Keith R. McFarland, who served as project director for the publication process, and to Bill Henegar and Brenda Seale for helping with all aspects of manuscript preparation and publication. Claudia Arnold and Patricia Yomantas provided professional guidance from Pepperdine University for staging the conference and arranging details with the speakers.

I am also grateful to Dr. Howard A. White, President of Pepperdine University, for his encouragement to stage this important series of lectures and to share it with a wider audience in published form.

That such a powerful idea as freedom should continue to haunt us after two hundred years is indicative of the fact that ours is a way of life which is yet youthful and energetic. As Victor Hugo has reminded us, nothing is more powerful than an idea whose time has come.

James R. Wilburn
Malibu, California
1982

Contributors

JAMES R. WILBURN

James R. Wilburn is vice-president and dean of the School of Business and Management and Professor of Economic History at Pepperdine University. At the university, he has also held positions as vice-president for University Affairs and executive assistant to the president, as well as provost and chief administrative officer of the Los Angeles campus. He is the author of several books, including a textbook on leadership and *The Hazard of the Die*, which received the McGarvey Award for its contribution to the understanding of American history. He has also written a biography of Marcus Hanna and a history of the World War II aircraft industry in Southern California. His essay, "The Search for Economic Liberty," was published by the Los Angeles County Almanac for 1979, and his speech, "The Entrepreneurial Imperative," received the 1980 George Washington Medal of Honor from the Freedoms Foundation of Valley Forge.

For ten years, Dr. Wilburn was president of a publishing firm before joining Pepperdine University. He received his Ph.D. from UCLA with undergraduate degrees from Abilene Christian University and Midwestern University. He was appointed by Ronald Reagan to be the president of the CFTR Education Foundation.

STEPHEN J. TONSOR

Stephen Tonsor is a professor of 19th century and contemporary European history at the University of Michigan and an adjunct scholar at the American Enterprise Institute of Public Policy Research, where he served during the 1980 academic year as a research fellow.

Dr. Tonsor earned his undergraduate and Ph.D. degrees at the University of Illinois, and later received the doctorate in literature at Blackburn College. He served on the faculties of the University of Zurich and the University of Munich before joining the department of history at the University of Michigan.

In 1972-73, Dr. Tonsor served as a senior visiting research fellow at the Hoover Institution, and is a former president of the Philadelphia Society. For three years he served as a consultant to the President's Council of Economic Advisers. He is the author of *Tradition and Reform in Education*, has been associate editor of *Modern Age* since 1970, and is currently at work on another book, *The History of the Idea of Equality*.

SIDNEY HOOK

Sidney Hook is a senior research fellow at the Hoover Institution on War, Revolution, and Peace at Stanford University. The recipient of three Guggenheim Fellowships for research in European philosophy, Dr. Hook won the Nicholas Murray Butler Silver Medal for distinction in the field of philosophy, upon the publication of his book, *Hero in History*. He was awarded a Ford Foundation Traveling Fellowship for the study of Asian philosophy and culture.

A graduate of Columbia University, where he earned the doctorate in philosophy after intensive study with John Dewey and F.J.E. Woodbridge, Dr. Hook's teaching assignments included posts at Columbia University, New York University, Harvard University, the University of California, and the New School for Social Research.

His numerous books and articles on education, philosophy, and politics include *Revolution, Reform and Social Justice; Education for Modern Man; Philosophy and Public Policy; Academic Freedom and Academic Anarchy;* and *Education and the Taming of Power.*

STANLEY L. JAKI

Stanley Jaki was the 1981 MacDonald Lecturer at the University of Sydney and a Distinguished University Professor at Seton Hall University, where he has been a faculty member since 1965. He was invited to deliver the prestigious Gifford Lectures at the University of Edinburgh, only the sixth American Gifford lecturer after William James, Josiah Royce, John Dewey, Paul Tillich, and Reinhold Niebuhr.

Born in Hungary, Dr. Jaki earned the doctorate in systematic theology at the Pontifical Institute in San Anselmo, and was ordained as a priest in 1948. He earned the Ph.D. at Fordham University under the tutelage of the late Nobel-laureate Dr. Victor F. Hess, who is credited with discovering the cosmic ray.

Dr. Jaki has done extensive research and teaching at Stanford University, the University of California at Berkeley, Princeton University, the St. Vincent School of Theology, and Balliol College of Oxford, and was elected in 1980 as the Hoyt Fellow at Yale University.

A prolific writer, Dr. Jaki has authored numerous books including *The Relevance of Physics, Cosmos and Creator, The Road of Science and the Ways of God*, and *Brain, Mind and Computers*, for which he was awarded the Lecompte du Nouy Prize in 1970.

ABRAHAM J. MALHERBE

Abraham Malherbe is the Buckingham Professor of New Testament Criticism and Interpretation at Yale University. Considered one of the most prominent and respected New Testament scholars of today, he is a specialist in the study of Christian origins, Patristics, Hellenistic philosophy and religion.

Born in Pretoria, South Africa, Dr. Malherbe majored in Greek at Abilene Christian University and earned bachelor's and doctoral degrees in theology at Harvard Divinity School. He pursued additional study in Hellenistic philosophy at the University of Utrecht in The Netherlands. He taught at Abilene Christian University, was a visiting scholar at Harvard Divinity School, and taught religion at Dartmouth College before accepting his permanent assignment at Yale in 1971.

Dr. Malherbe has authored several scholarly works, including *The World of the New Testament; Social Aspects of Early Christianity; The Cynic Epistles: A Study Edition;* and *The Life of Moses.* He was presented the Christian Research Publications Award in 1967 for his translation of *Di Vita Moysis,* and was named the Rockwell Lecturer at Rice University in 1975.

MICHAEL NOVAK

Michael Novak is a resident scholar in religion, philosophy, and public policy at the American Enterprise Institute in Washington, D.C., and former Ledden-Watson Distinguished Professor of Religion at Syracuse University. In 1981 he represented the United States at the 37th session of the United Nations Commission on Human Rights in Geneva, Switzerland.

Dr. Novak graduated from Holy Cross Seminary, Stonehill College, the Gregorian University in Rome, Catholic University, and Harvard University. He has taught at Harvard, at Old Westbury of the State of New York, and at Stanford University, where consecutive senior classes elected him the "Most Influential Professor" during two of his three years on the faculty.

Dr. Novak's books, eighteen published in as many years in every Western language, include *The Rise of the Unmeltable Ethnics; Belief and Unbelief; Ascent of the Mountain, Flight of the Dove; The Theology of the Corporation;* and *Capitalism and Socialism: A Theological Inquiry.* His most recent is *The Spirit of Democratic Capitalism,* published in 1982.

GEORGE GILDER

George Gilder is the program director of the International Center for Economic Policy Studies and author of the best-selling book, *Wealth and Poverty.* He has been actively involved in the formulation of "supply-side" economics since the early 1970's, as chairman of the Economic Roundtable at the Lehrman Institute in New York City.

A graduate of Harvard University where he studied sociology and government, Mr. Gilder and a Harvard classmate launched a quarterly magazine entitled *Advance.* His speech-writing career included work for Nelson Rockefeller and Jacob Javits. He spent a year as a junior fellow on the Council of Foreign Relations, and was a legislative assistant to Maryland Senator Charles Mathias. He also served on the Harvard faculty and earned a fellowship to the Kennedy Institute of Politics.

A former editor of *New Leader* and *The Ripon Forum*, Mr. Gilder is the author of *Visible Man*, *Sexual Suicide*, and *The Party that Lost Its Head*. He is a regular contributor to such leading publications as *The Wall Street Journal*, *Harper's Magazine*, *The Washington Post* and *National Review*, and lectures extensively throughout the United States and Europe.

HENRY G. MANNE

Henry Manne is director of the Law and Economics Center at Emory University, where he is a professor at the University's School of Law. He served for six years as director of the Law and Economics Center at the University of Miami.

Dr. Manne completed his undergraduate education in economics at Vanderbilt University, and earned the juris doctor degree at the University of Chicago Law School. Following advanced graduate studies at Yale University, he was awarded the LL.M. and J.S.D. degrees. He holds membership in the Illinois and New York Bar Associations and the American Bar Association, and is admitted to practice before the United States Supreme Court.

The author of numerous books and articles, Dr. Manne's publications include *Insider Trading and the Stock Market*; *Gold, Money and the Law*; *The Modern Corporation and Social Responsibility*; *Wall Street in Transition*; and *The Economics of Legal Relationships*.

RUSSELL KIRK

Russell Kirk, author, columnist, and historian, is the author of twenty-three books, of which more than one million copies have been sold. Among his most widely read volumes are *The Conservative Mind*, one of this century's seminal works on political theory, which evoked an eight-page cover story in Time magazine, and *The Roots of American Order*, published by Pepperdine University Press.

Dr. Kirk received his undergraduate education at Michigan State University, his master's degree at Duke University, and the doctor of letters (earned) from St. Andrews, as the only American to hold the highest arts degree of the senior Scottish University. A professor for many years at Long Island University, he has been named a distinguished visiting professor at several institutions, including Pepperdine University, was a Guggenheim Fellow and a senior fellow of the American Council of Learned Societies. He is the editor of the influential quarterly, *The University Bookman,* and was the founding editor of *Modern Age.* He earned the Christopher Award for his book, *Eliot and His Age,* and the Ann Radcliffe Award of the Count Dracula Society for his gothic fiction.

Chapter 1

The Indivisibility
of Freedom

JAMES R. WILBURN

"The university is a marketplace for ideas." That was a
favorite quotation of Dr. Franklin Murphy in the
1960's when he was Chancellor of the University of California
at Los Angeles and I was a graduate student there.

I thought the analogy was a good one. An intellectual
"marketplace" implies that students have access to competing
ideas, free to choose those which survive the clash of debate
and the exposure of analysis. The most sacred icons either melt
away or are purified in the fire of full investigation.

The concept of a free market also recognizes our potential for
intelligent choices and encourages our basic instinct toward
freedom. Honoring the individual's right to choose among
competing ideas, lifestyles, and products enhances the quality
of life and celebrates human worth, dignity, and intelligence.
The analogy of a free market is especially poignant for educators
because knowledge multiplies options and options expand
freedom. The university should be a "marketplace for ideas."

The same campus where this slogan was honored took on the
charged atmosphere of a battlefield at sunrise on the day of an
historic conflict when some students and faculty decided that
other students and faculty should be denied their freedom to

enter the ROTC building or to meet with recruiters from a large corporation to apply for employment. Disruptive marchers plagued professors who conscientiously refused to dismiss their classes to join the festivities. Hundreds of armed troops were necessary to guarantee the university regents their freedom to meet on campus. The angry mob decided that Ronald Reagan, as governor and regent of the university, did not deserve freedom to assemble with other regents.

I was disturbed by the glaring contradiction. Insisting on freedom for one person's ideas but not for another's seemed as blatantly inconsistent to me then as it does now. Freedom, it seemed to me, was a whole fabric. Demanding freedom for me but not for you or allowing freedom of speech but not freedom of assembly seemed to rip the fabric into pieces and thus to destroy the essence of freedom itself.

Often when we commit to what we believe is a self-evident truth, we do not realize that our commitment may take us far beyond what we thought was ultimate. When the American colonies hurled their slogans of freedom at the king of England to declare their intentions of independence, many did not realize that the same idea of freedom, once uncaged, would return to ravage some of their own honored institutions, such as slavery.

The American Revolution continued to simmer and boil over again and again, stirred by the indivisibility of "freedom's ferment." It overwhelmed the state church in Virginia. Fifty years following the war for independence from England, it disestablished the church in New England, launching the nation on a historic and bold new experiment in the separation of church and state. It moved the nation inexorably toward the Civil War to abolish slavery. Still later, it engulfed the prejudice which denied women the right to vote and blacks a seat at the front of the bus. The Revolutionary leaders in Boston would have been shocked if they could have divined how far their enthusiasm for freedom would carry the nation in only two brief centuries.[1]

In my judgment, those of us privileged to participate in this exciting experiment in freedom are still watching an unfinished revolution, for our civilization is yet an infant. America's current renaissance of awareness may discover afresh the spiritual, intellectual, and philosophical roots of economic freedom. Especially those who urge that a university campus should provide a free market for ideas, if they are prepared to follow that principle further, must recognize the close relationship of free markets of every sort, including free economic exchanges between consenting adults. If we take seriously the passion for political freedom which fueled the civil-rights marches of the 1960's, we are forced to understand that the destinies of political freedom and economic freedom are strategically and inevitably joined. The leaders of the civil-rights movement understood the relationship in their bones. To deny the right to hold personal property or to deny economic reward for creative effort is to deny human worth just as surely as the denial of political rights. Freedom, whether spiritual, economic, political, or intellectual, is indivisible.[2]

This indivisibility of freedom is demonstrated daily in the academic world where it is the underlying principle supporting the concept of tenure. The most effective tool for silencing academic freedom is the threat to economic welfare. The economic guarantees of tenure ensure intellectual freedom so that no one can deny my right to earned wages simply because I express an unpopular idea.[3]

The principle of academic freedom should also extend to the student. We have all known a charismatic professor whose crusading spirit and engaging personality tempted him to exploit students who at a most impressionable age were looking for something different and whose potential for moral indignation was at a higher level in college than in younger years. The professor's immersion in his own specialty can easily overpower students who are not adequately trained in critical analysis and evaluation. The potential travesty of cognitive freedom is further aggravated by the tendency of academic departments to hire and offer tenure to professors who mirror the biases of the majority school of thought already represented in the department. Exposed to a relatively homogeneous set of beliefs, students mistake indoctrination for emancipation, exchange one set of biases for another, and fail to develop the cognitive skills of true academic freedom. To manipulate the intellectual direction of students is as much a denial of academic freedom as is a heavy-handed administration or a legislature which levies economic sanctions against a professor with unpopular political beliefs.

To illustrate the indivisibility of freedom in another set, the discipline of economics was formerly referred to as "political economics," a description still preferred by many and a perception of human behavior closer to the real world. One example of this relationship between economic and political systems is found in our century's experiments in democratic socialism and democratic capitalism. While the free market of capitalism reflects a respect for the individual's freedom to use his personal resources as he chooses, the voting booth of democracy recognizes the individual's freedom to allocate his political resources as he decides. Democracy and capitalism are two expressions of the same principle, making "democratic capitalism" an apt description of America's system.

"Democratic socialism," on the other hand, is turning out to be a contradiction in terms. It is based on the false assumption that the state can own and control property (the means of production) without controlling political and intellectual resources as well. Sixty years ago, when socialism presented such a profoundly compassionate vision of a world of universal brotherhood, we might have been so optimistic. The appeal of socialism was religious, calling for a new social order based upon "new men and women" who were to turn their backs on the moral flaws of the real world, lured on by a sincere hope that humankind would soon shed the character traits imputed to it by the book of Genesis. Predicting the twilight of capitalism with its evil dollar-sign symbol, its bloated bankers, and its three-martini business lunches, socialism fed on the idealism of its disciples.

Now after more than fifty years of experience with socialist states, we are no longer forced to depend on rhetoric alone. Everywhere, life under socialism has turned out to be a record of words that succeed marvelously but policies that fail miserably.[4]

Aside from the totalitarian and expansionist obessions of the Soviet Union, there is the utter and complete failure of socialism in Britain, Scandinavia, and such hopeful, emerging nations as Tanzania. Captivated by the alluring falsehood that nationalization of industries means control by "the people," the British almost overnight lost their once-proud position of leadership to a debilitated economy, chaotic political institutions, and the loss of national will which attends economic decline (since freedoms are indivisible).

Sweden is an even more compelling example. Alva Myrdal, wife of Gunnar Myrdal, the leading intellectual sponsor of the Swedish welfare state, noted in 1932, "The Scandinavian countries, and particularly Sweden, have by historical accident been given the most advantageous set of prerequisites for a bold experiment in social democracy (i.e., social welfarism). . . . If it could not develop successfully in Scandinavia it will probably not work anywhere else."[5]

American intellectuals have long delighted in pointing to Sweden as the place where democratic socialism has worked. Yet, sadly and finally, it has not worked there either. Government expenditures have risen to about 68 percent of GNP, which has been stagnant for the past decade. Organized labor has made such demands for security that even a liquidated company must, by law, guarantee employees six months full pay. Since this reserve must be deposited up front when firms are being formed, numerous new ventures which could be launched are not formed at all, destroying one of the most creative, productive, and innovative sectors of society and ultimately denying citizens a higher quality of life.

An employee in Sweden who works half-time qualifies for full state-guaranteed social benefits. The result is a higher tax on the earnings of workers than anywhere else in the world. Because every family of four is guaranteed $12,000 annually, the marginal tax on earnings up to that amount is 100 percent. Taxes on an income of $20,000 effectively cut spendable income to $12,000. There is no incentive for the individual earning $5,000 to attempt to earn $20,000, for there would be no benefit. In both cases, net spendable income would be $12,000.

There is little wonder that this once-vigorous nation experienced a tragic decline of nearly 25 percent in the average annual working time in industry between 1960 and 1978. At the same time, absenteeism rose by 60 percent. The underground economy of unreported (thus untaxed) income is surging, with its inevitable chilling effect on moral sensitivity. Gunnar Myrdal himself has finally lamented, "The tax system is turning

Swedes into a gang of hustlers . . . The present tax system is making nine out of ten Swedes criminals."[6]

Others have pointed to the system of codetermination in West Germany, where the results of the growing power of labor have yet to become totally clear. Many German industries now controlled by labor, however, are in serious economic difficulty. Able observers believe that equal representation by employees on boards of directors in the coal and steel industries helps to account for the fact that the miracle of German economic recovery after World War II never touched those industries. Parity codetermination has certainly not produced peace in the labor market. Beyond these failures are the moral and ideological implications of political seizure of property for redistribution to those who do not bear the risk of management.[7]

Thus, as economic freedom and intellectual freedom are mutually dependent, so are economic freedom and political freedom. Because socialism separates the two, even its best form is ineffective and impoverishing. Its worst form is totalitarian.

Democratic capitalism, though more successful in distributing wealth and sharing political power, has failed to stir the hearts of potential converts as deeply as has socialism. This failure is true partly because capitalists have been reluctant to promise so much. A free American press has made them vulnerable to a microscopic review which would be incomprehensible to the closed institutions of a socialist society.

In spite of its timid claims, democratic capitalism has made historic contributions to millions from every corner of the world. Yet in one of the most ironic twists of human history, its very success has presented it with a moral crisis which may be its undoing. In his classical work *Capitalism, Socialism, and Democracy* Joseph A. Schumpeter demonstrated that capitalism's incredible efficiency in creating wealth incubates its own destruction.[8] An ever-rising standard of living and increased leisure can focus on a life which is without meaning. Discovering that the gold ring entitles us to nothing more than another ride on the merry-go-round, we confuse our own self-delusion with a conspiracy by the system to deceive us. If this emptiness is magnified by the envious resentments of individuals who participate unequally in a secular improvement which is taken for granted by the majority, the seeds for destroying the system and ourselves with it are nourished to life.

In addition to the efficiencies of capitalism is the threat which technology has always posed to established ideas and class relationships, including comfortable expressions of order and morality. Democratic capitalism has tended to fracture these structures, permitting aggressive entrepreneurs to clamber up through the cracks, sometimes without proper reverence for social order. Even Irving Kristol, usually considered a friend and defender, has offered only "Two Cheers for Capitalism," reserving the third because of the over-emphasis on consumption and sensual gratification which results from the "spiritual vacuum at the center of our free and capitalistic society."[9]

Both socialist and capitalist idealists, who tend to confuse their longing and suspected potential for Utopia with an achievable reality, are predestined to disenchantment. William Barrett, discussing the stages of disillusionment with socialism which he and other Twentieth Century intellectuals have experienced, has noted that "a great deal of antagonism toward capitalism historically has come out of the unrecognized need to satisfy other and more obscure gropings." For many, the socialist ideal represents "a displacement of moral and religious values which had not found their outlet elsewhere and here came to distorted expression." Barrett further notes that in the socialist tradition "you can scarcely disentangle specific social protest from a metaphysical rebellion against, *or evasion of* the human condition itself" (Emphasis mine — JRW).[10]

Evading the realities of the human predicament while pursuing blind dreams of Utopia is a common theme among socialist writers. I personally followed, with great admiration, the dreams of Julius Nyerere in the years preceding the final autonomy of his homeland, Tanzania. His autobiographical collection of essays and speeches, *Not Yet Uhuru,* was a moving depiction of courage and hope. Now, to witness the agony and bitter disillusionment which has accompanied his valiant effort to erect a viable socialist nation has been to watch a modern tragedy of heroic proportions.

In spite of these faiures the socialist myth retains great power over Western intellectuals. But Peter L. Berger suggests an antidote:

There is, however, one fairly effective remedy against the power of the socialist myth — the experience of living in a society where that myth has been politically elevated to the status of official doctrine. One of the savage ironies of the times is that, ideologically, Marxism is on the ascendancy everywhere — *except* in the countries that call themselves Marxist. One cannot lure a cat from behind the chimney with Marxist rhetoric in the Soviet Union or in Eastern Europe. There Marxism is ceremony, the myth has become a petrified ornament. On the basis of that empirical evidence, one prediction is fairly certain: Western intellectuals will cease to be fascinated by the socialist myth soon after Western societies are taken over by socialist regimes. It must be added, however, than in the not improbable case that these regimes will resemble Soviet totalitarianism, this belated conversion will have little, if any, political significance. For totalitarian regimes, it appears, can survive for a long time without plausible myths and in a cultural climate of pervasive cynicism.

There is one more possibility: a reversal of the long-standing trend of secularization in the Western world generally, and particularly in its cultural elite.[11]

The failure of socialism leads to the importance of spiritual freedom for those entrusted with the institutions of economic and political freedom, which have been highly successful in a material way. It is possible for such a society, denied a powerful religious mythology of profound meaning, to decay for lack of moral purpose. How democratic capitalism handles the moral crisis which it faces will determine whether or not it holds together and provides structure for individual fulfillment or flies apart from its own centrifugal momentum because it lacks the inner cohesion of a moral and spiritual core. Intellectual, economic, and political freedoms can be harnassed, disciplined, and directed only if they maintain their sustaining tie to the spiritual freedom which nourished them to life and to strength.

To insist that spiritual freedom belongs with economic, political, and intellectual freedom it not to deny that capitalism has sometimes permitted human exploitation. It is to maintain that exploitation and materialist values are neither inherent to

8

nor more common under capitalism than under socialism. For every Great Gatsby, George Babbitt, or Willy Loman there is a health agent in a Soviet hospital who plays the role of a little god (most recently portrayed by Saul Bellow in *The Dean's December*). We have also learned of the inhumane results of socialism through writers such as Alexander Solzhenitsyn.

Further, there are many people living under economic and political totalitarianism who are nevertheless able to maintain a freedom of the soul which is inspiring. Many such people in the Soviet Union and the People's Republic of China, sustained by a deep faith, worship freely even though they have no political voice. The apostle Paul had perhaps his greatest spiritual impact while he was a prisoner in Rome, including his conversion of Onesimus, who though a slave found his own spiritual freedom through his faith and his "enslavement" to Christ (becoming a servant to his fellow man).

In his poem "To Althea, From Prison" Richard Lovelace captured a similar understanding:

> Stone walls do not a prison make,
>   Nor iron bars a cage;
> Minds innocent and quiet take
>   That for an hermitage;
> If I have freedom in my love
>   And in my soul am free,
> Angels alone, that soar above,
>   Enjoy such liberty.

One of the most moving experiences of my life was my visit to the tiny attic in Amsterdam where Anne Frank and her family survived for several years until the Nazis discovered them and took them to prison and to death. The diary of Anne Frank is a classic monument to the freedom of the human spirit, undaunted even by her self-imposed prison.

The inherent tension which spiritual freedom creates when denied physical freedom illustrates profoundly that freedom is indivisible. Economic and political freedoms are related to spiritual freedom in the same sense in which a tree is indivisible from its roots. Intellectual freedom, economic freedom, and political freedom are the fruit of man's spiritual nature and a logical result of his yearning for spiritual fulfillment.

To say that freedom should be indivisible is not to say that it is ultimate or total. One person's pursuit of freedom can lead to the exploitation of another person's individuality. The authors of the United States Constitution, for instance, to honor the inviolability of private property protected the institution of slavery. They inconsistently denied freedom to black slaves in order to guarantee the unlimited economic freedom of others. Similarly, freedom of speech does not include the right to shout "fire" in a crowded theater or to damage another person's reputation through slander.

In the delicate balance of free democratic institutions, however, this limitation of liberty must first of all be a voluntary moral self-restraint which honors the rights of others. Otherwise, selfish claims on liberty can destroy society's order. If enough individuals lose confidence in the system or if there no longer exists a critical mass of people who are guided by an inner moral gyroscope to honor the freedom of others out of genuine concern and respect, then we cannot hire enough policemen or pass enough laws to keep society together. As Solzhenitsyn has noted, the proliferation of lawyers and our national binge of legal action is a barometer measuring the falling inner pressure of our moral self-restraint. An effective way to destroy a free society is for enough individuals to press their "rights," demanding personal liberty without moral responsibility, until the society turns to the Strong Man to bring order once again. Adolf Hitler rose to power in a democracy which was suffering from insecurity and confusion. Ironically, the totalitarian temptation is at both ends of freedom's spectrum.[12]

Understanding the indivisibility of human freedom has important consequences for higher education. It can unify the disparate and diverse disciplines of the university's curriculum and provide a single conduit through some of the profoundest realities of human experience. Without that understanding, the multitude of students and faculty of the modern university share little that is more significant than a common purse and a common parking lot. But freedom gathers significant endeavors from all the professions, engages the scholarly yearning of the research laboratory, and in the university fuses them into an institutional form which has proven to be one of the most durable structures of human history.

Amid the wreck and crash of worlds and the groans of one culture giving way to the next, freedom matters, and it matters to all.

This focus brings more to the university than mere cohesion. It also brings significance. Human freedom stresses that individuals are morally responsible for their actions.

This theme engages one of the most important discussions of our age. The centuries-long debate about moral responsibility is yoked to the myriad theories about human nature which cluster around the magnetic poles of either free will or determinism. In Augustine, Aquinas, Henry James, Tolstoy, Dostoevsky, and Camus, determinism has taken many forms through the centuries, usually theological in nature. More recent expressions have tended to use secular categories, including the escape from responsibility implied by the Freudian concept of the subconscious. Such a subtlety as changing the personal pronoun from the nominative to the possessive, from "I" to "my," can signal a tidal shift in attitude toward moral responsibility. If it is "my" *id* which is to blame, then it is not "I." That moral assumption has infused modern literature, social institutions, and court decisions.

Also gravitating toward the deterministic pole is the whole behavioral movement which has dominated much of American thought since the 1920's. It has made considerable contributions not only to psychology but to political science, economics, anthropology, sociology, law, and most recently, to the new science of sociobiology.[13] Its best known and most popular spokesman is B.F. Skinner. Dr. Skinner's deep sincerity in laying the psychological foundations for a better world is obvious. He asserts, however, that the concept of an "autonomous man" is self-deluding and mythical, invented to impress ourselves that we have mastery over our own destiny. While he maintains that we are free to some degree, not always clear to us, he defines freedom as man's effort to escape bad consequences and avoid noxious conditions. Because these urges have genetic roots, taken alone they can be interpreted as part of a deterministic scheme.[14]

Obviously, environmental stimuli can have a major impact on behavior. Yet Skinner's own strong hope for changing the world is hardly compatible with the perfect passivity into which the more trendy world of complete environmental determinism could easily seduce us. Most disturbing is Skinner's failure to identify which technocrats are to be the guardians of the public good, to decide which of our contingencies are to be reinforced and which are to be discouraged. Although he abhors the horror of Orwell's 1984 as much as anyone else, his own version of a future Utopia would still curtail the activities of advertising experts in the mass media. Such a denial of freedom is necessary, Skinner maintains, since the experts condition people to demand worthless products. The sobering question remains: who decides which products are worthless?

The opposite pole of the human-nature question has gathered impressive evidence for man's free will. In fact, Skinner's scheme of survival through conditioned response becomes increasingly suspect in a period of technological future shock and rapid political and cultural change. As most of his critics have noted, Skinner extrapolates from the experience of pigeons in a controlled environment to draw fundamental conclusions about human beings who face a variety of unpredictable stimuli. In an uncontrolled environment, responses are uncertain, unique, and often not repeatable. It is rather differentiation of response and the ability to evaluate consequences which are the keys to coping successfully with unexpected circumstances. Perpetual uncertainty in human experience requires unpredictability in the response.

Extinguishing a person's belief in his own autonomy can make him so passive as to exhibit symptoms of psychosis, like some caged animal or prison inmate. If this paralysis disables the human spirit through an entire age, the results can be catastrophic. Survival, now more than ever before, requires freedom.

Nowhere is this principle more important than in the university where human freedom is implied by the very existence of our educational system. We teach in order to enlarge knowledge about options. Variety of possibilities underscores man's capacity for creative choice and focuses on his powers of reason. Beyond these considerations, the very habit of reflective thought, surely a purposive choice rather than a reflexive impulse, is an even more autonomous decision than rational action itself.

Creating a chain of unique choices, moments of self-questioning and pondered plans, leads to a major objective of the entire educational process — namely, creative problem solving. Creativity will always remain bothersome to determinists because they have no logic for explaining the person who chooses to challenge received wisdom and to produce something which, after the fact, is obvious and practical and at the moment of creation new and unpredictable.

The apparent contradiction between freedom and a university based on some degree of commitment to a specific set of beliefs is solved by some apologists through encouraging a pluralism of commitments or beliefs. A more attractive solution is based on the principle of humility and tolerance for students' intelligent questionings. A value-centered education should be under the guardianship of individuals who unashamedly profess a commitment of faith. Yet if they curtail investigation, they reveal their own suspicion that their faith will not survive examination. Attitudes of compassion, humility, and honesty communicate far more effectively than creedal statements. Humility acknowledges that no human institutional expression of faith is ultimate, thus beyond questioning. Any institution which demands such loyalty is guilty of idolatry.

If academic freedom, like economic and political freedom, is grounded in spiritual freedom, then professors and students alike are responsible for their priorities, their decisions, and their actions. This essential assumption of freedom as the foundation of education itself continues to gather ample evidence as the decades march by. Albert Einstein's theory of the nature of time and space, portraying a universe where time is curved, and the more recent physics of quantum mechanics, which admits to unlimited alternate realities at each moment of consciousness, hint at a resolution of the old debate over the foreknowledge of God and man's free choice. These surprising changes in the direction of scientific thought also place the freedom of choice among options squarely in the hands of an intelligent, autonomous, self-aware individual. Add to this Werner Heisenberg's principle of indeterminacy and we realize that quantum theory has shoved contemporary man beyond the classical, the medieval, and the modern world to a new physics and philosophy. Anyone who stubbornly continues to make an epistemological idol of the closed, Cartesian world of the "scientific method" is still living under the faith of a previous century.[15]

Human freedom justifies the excitement of the university's most sacred ventures. It endows the classroom with heavy responsibilities. But its indivisibility insists that those who commit to intellectual freedom must also honor economic freedom. And those who find political freedom to be their most sanguine motivation must understand that political freedom and economic freedom both speak finally of the yearning for spiritual freedom.

If we move away from this central understanding, discovered through millennia of serious searching by our forebears and confirmed by the newly revealed bits and pieces of information which provide the clues of succeeding centuries, it is not because we have discovered something new about ourselves. It is rather because we have momentarily forgotten essentially who we are. The thrill of it all is that each time we rediscover our spiritual identity we understand that our need for freedom, properly defined and understood, can endow not only the curriculum but the university itself with meaningful structure. The renewal of that constantly recurring self-discovery can also recover the passion which makes the life of the teacher worthwhile.

NOTES

1. Alice Felt Tyler, *Freedom's Ferment* (New York: Harper & Row, 1962). This social history traces American reform movements, and their close relationship to revivalism and to each other, from Colonial times to the outbreak of the Civil War. For the most recent and thorough study of the impact of the American Revolution on the nation's attitude toward slavery, see Willie Lee Rose (ed., William W. Freehling), *Slavery and Freedom* (New York: Oxford University Press, 1982). This collection of Mrs. Rose's essays includes two important pieces on the considerable impact on slavery of the American Revolution. As she demonstrates, the inconsistency between the war's justification of "life, liberty and happiness" and the institution of slavery produced a far-reaching crisis for the national conscience.

2. The occasion for the lectures contained in this volume was a faculty conference based on one statement from the institutional affirmation, printed in the front of all university catalogs and in each graduation program of Pepperdine University:

"Pepperdine University Affirms . . .

THAT GOD IS,

That He is revealed uniquely in Christ;

That the educational process may not, with impunity, be divorced from the divine process;

That the student, as a person of infinite dignity, is the heart of the educational enterprise;

That the quality of student life is a valid concern of the University;

That truth, having nothing to fear from investigation, must be pursued relentlessly in every discipline;

That spiritual commitment, tolerating no excuse for mediocrity, demands the highest standards of academic excellence;

That freedom, whether spiritual, intellectual, or economic, is indivisible;

That knowledge calls, ultimately, for a life of service."

3. American Association of University Professors, *Faculty Tenure: A Report and Recommendations by the Commission on Academic Tenure in Higher Education* (San Francisco: Jossey-Bass Publishers, 1973); Bardwell L. Smith, *et al.*, *The Tenure Debate* (San Francisco: Jossey-Bass Publishers, 1973); Nathan Glazer, "The Torment of Tenure," in Sidney Hook (ed.), *The Idea of a Modern University* (Buffalo, New York: Prometheus Books, 1974); George C. Roche, III, *Education in America* (Irvington-on-Hudson, New York: The Foundation of Economic Education, 1969), pp. 96-119; Russell Kirk, *Academic Freedom* (Chicago: Henry Regnery Company, 1955).

4. Murray Edelman, *Political Language: Words That Succeed and Policies That Fail* (New York: Academic Press, 1977).

5. Quoted in Arthur Shenfield, *The Failure of Socialism: Learning from the Swedes and English* (Washington, D.C.: The Heritage Foundation, 1980), p. 23. I am also indebted to Dr. Shenfield for the statistics on the national economy of Sweden. See also Roland Hunford, *The New Totalitarians* (Scarborough House in Briarcliff, New York: Stein & Day, 1980); Sven Rydenfelt, "The Limits of Taxation: Lessons from the Swedish Welfare State," a paper presented to the Mont Pelerin Society Meeting at Stanford University, September, 1980.

6. Shenfield, p. 16. For a recent treatment of socialism, democracy and capitalism, see Michael Novak, *The Spirit of Democratic Capitalism* (New York: Simon & Schuster, 1982); Michael Novak (ed.), *Capitalism and Socialism: A Theological Enquiry* (Washington, D.C.: American Enterprise Institute, 1979); Paul C. Goelz (ed.), *An Economic Philosophy for a Free People* (San Antonio: St. Mary's University Press, 1979).

7. Steve Pejovich, *Codetermination in the West: The Case of Germany* (Washington, D.C.: The Heritage Foundation, 1982). Walter Hamm, *Erfahrungen mit der Mitbestimmung in der Bundesrepublik Deutschland*, Schweizerischer Handels-und Industrie-Verein, #25, September, 1981, cited by Hans F. Sennholz, "Codetermination in West Germany," *The Freeman*, 32:1 (January, 1982), 15-22.

8. (New York: Harper & Row, 1942), pp. 59-164.

9. Irving Kristol, *Two Cheers for Capitalism* (New York: Basic Books, Inc., 1978). See also Robert Wuthnour, "The Moral Crisis in American Capitalism," *Harvard Business Review*, 60:2 (March-April, 1982) 76-84.

10. William Barrett was one of twenty-six writers asked by the editors of *Commentary* to address the question of the connection between capitalism and democracy in *Commentary*, 65:4 (April, 1978). The responses were later published by the American Enterprise Institute as *Capitalism, Socialism and Democracy*.

11. *Facing Up to Modernity, Excursions in Society, Politics and Religion* (New York: Basic Books, 1977), p. 68.

12. Jean-Francois Revel, *The Totalitarian Temptation*, trans. David Hapgood (Garden City, New York: Doubleday & Company, 1977).

13. Edmond Ions, *Against Behaviorism: A Critique of Behavioral Science* (Oxford: Basil Blackwell, 1977), pp. 126-133; Merle Curti, *Human Nature in America* (Madison: The University of Wisconsin Press, 1980), pp. 372-406; Edward O. Wilson, *On Human Nature* (Cambridge: Harvard University Press, 1978).

14. Finley Carpenter, *The Skinner Primer: Beyond Freedom and*

Dignity (New York: The Free Press, 1974), pp. 85-99, 176-214.

15. Werner Heisenberg, *Physics and Philosophy* (New York: Harper & Row, 1958); Gary Zukav, *The Dancing Wu Li Masters: An Overview of the New Physics* (New York: McGraw-Hill, 1979); Frank Capra, *The Tao of Physics* (Berkeley: Shambala, 1975); Heinz R. Pagels, *The Cosmic Code: Quantum Physics as the Language of Nature* (New York: Simon and Schuster, 1982); Fred Alan Wolf, *Taking the Quantum Leap* (San Francisco: Harper & Row, 1981).

Chapter 2

Why Democratic Technocrats Need the Liberal Arts

STEPHEN J. TONSOR

Periodically in the United States there is a return to Liberal Arts education. The free elective system and an emphasis on vocational training are abandoned and the old-time religion of the Liberal Arts once more comes into vogue. Indeed it might be more realistic to argue that the conception of Liberal Arts education has, for a very long time, been the norm and that the free elective system and vocational training are deviations made in spite of the traditional wisdom.

The United States in 1981 seems to have entered a period when the Liberal Arts tradition is once more in the ascendant. In nearly every major university and in most colleges, curriculum committees are once more considering and instituting required courses and broad Liberal Arts surveys, and college faculties are debating both the wisdom and the means of restoring a Liberal Arts curriculum. After a decade of educational *laissez faire* the visible hand of deans and faculties rather than the invisible hand of student popular demand has become the determining factor in shaping and guiding curricular development.

It is a recurring pattern, and one might, if one were cynical, ask whether it means anything at all other than that intellectuals are as deeply enslaved to fashion and faddishness as any group

19

in our society and that dropping the foreign language requirement is like dropping the hem-line.

I will not argue with those who say that many intellectuals are silly faddists. I am afraid it is all too true. I do wish, however, to raise the question of whether there may not be reasons other than faddishness for the current revival of the Liberal Arts curriculum and I do wish to explore with you the perennial values of Liberal Arts education.

About forty years ago when I was serving in the army in World War II, it was often said that there were no "atheists in fox-holes." That is to say, that when men are in life and death situations belief and faith become important elements in their survival. As William James long ago said in his essay on "The Sentiment of Rationality,"

> Suppose, for example, that I am climbing in the Alps and have the ill luck to work myself into a position from which the only escape is a terrible leap. Being without similar experience, I have no evidence of my ability to perform it successfully, but hope and confidence in myself make me sure I shall not miss my aim, and nerve my feet to execute what without those subjective emotions would perhaps have been impossible. . . [1]

No doubt the desperate case produces believers whatever other grounds for faith may exist. And so too it is the desperate educational case which is responsible for the return to the old-time religion of the Liberal Arts. It is precisely the failure of training in contrast to education that has led to a renewed demand for a curriculum which will liberate and humanize, which will enable the student to deal with the demands of a complex technology and a complicated world with sophistication, comprehension and discrimination, and finally, which will temper mechanical skills with grace, art and moral sensitivity.

Put quite simply, we live in a world which needs experts of all sorts. At the lowest level we need people who can read and write, who are capable of reasoned thought and disciplined effort. About 25% of our fellow citizens do not possess the minimal literacy necessary to fill out an application for welfare. They are all but unemployable. The tasks to which the society will put them are, of necessity, menial and the political role which they will assume is that of passive receptor rather than active participant. They can not be fully men and they can not be free until they have become fully literate.

But why, in this instance, talk about the Liberal Arts; why not a Texas Instruments electronic teaching machine or an induction into Basic English via crime comics which will provide the minimal skills, higher than which these unfortunates can not reach?

The answer, of course, is that basic skills of this sort, the ability to read highway signs, for example, can not and will not liberate and humanize. Indeed they can not even provide the level of skills needed for success in the most ordinary pursuits of everyday life. I have been increasingly struck by the inability of ordinary men and women in television interviews to articulate their ideas, to express their hopes and fears, and to verbalize their emotions. Like Calaban they are slaves in a world they do not fully comprehend and even their hostilities and passions are inchoate and unexpressed. Are these the citizens of a republic?

Every living language, every mother tongue is first of all a language which has been spoken by poets who have given it its form and provided it with its symbolic subtlety and its nuanced expression. A language is only as adequate as its great poets are adequate. Those of you who have tried your hands at translating one language into another, especially at translating poetry, know that some languages succeed where others fail. This is as true of the language of mathematics and representational art as it is true of verbal expression. Czeslaw Milosz, the great Polish poet who this year won the Nobel prize wrote:

You asked me what is the good of reading
    the Gospels in Greek.
I answer that it is proper that we move our finger
Along letters more enduring than those carved in stone,
And that, slowly pronouncing each syllable
We discover the true dignity of speech.[2]

It is the poet who has given us "the true dignity of speech" but it is also the poet who gives us the subtlety of language necessary for expressing the intellectual complexity of the world in which we live.

No one can teach a language well who is estranged from or unacquainted with the poets of the language. What the ancients and the men of the Middle Ages called Rhetoric is one of the essential humanistic disciplines. It is essential to the ordinary college student for whom it is the key to understanding and knowledge, to scientific enquiry and precise description. Without an exact sense of language, without a precise description of things as they are, or as they might be, philosophy, law, and natural science are impossible. Without a poetry which touches the human heart and exactly describes the human condition, religion is dead and the emotions stultified.

But rhetoric is even more essential to the ordinary man or woman in our society who does not or cannot attend a college or university. Western men and women have had a 2,000 year training in the greatest "rhetoric," the language of the Bible, which mankind has available to it. As an educational source one of the most important aspects of the Bible is the fact that it speaks to all men indiscriminately: high and low, rich and poor, wise and foolish, sophisticated and ignorant, powerful and weak. It does not talk down to them but speaks in the accents of the Divine and in the language of the greatest poetry. The mind of Western man has been shaped by the language of that book. Like the Liberal Arts, the Bible has been successful in forming a culture because it reaches beyond its ostensible purpose (in the case of the Bible in conveying the Word of God), and informs and inspires a whole culture.

How startling and saddening it is, then, when one makes a Biblical allusion in a lecture and reads on the faces of the audience a look of blank incomprehension. One has the impression suddenly that one's contemporaries have become two-dimensional men, that the depth of the Scriptures is not one of their dimensions.

But in the absence of the Liberal Arts this happens not only in matters scriptural and religious but in the whole allusive language of great poetry and literature. I have the experience often in speaking to undergraduates that I have walked into a large unfurnished or badly furnished room. There is no place there for the soul's ease, no appropriate setting for intellectual or social intercourse, no stove in which to cook the simplest intellectual fare. As Gertrude Stein observed, "When you get there, there is no there there."

Instead of the exactly right word, instead of the precise and uncolored definition, instead of the poetic utterance one hears such phrases as "like, you know," or "I mean." Such substitutes for language are as my friend the late Martin Diamond said, "linguistic black holes" into which the meaning of the language is sucked and disappears. One is tempted to ridicule the poor, literally dumb student who uses such meaningless words, or shout as Jesus did when he healed the dumb man, "Be thou opened." But, alas, the only way that we can heal them is by teaching the Bible, the poets, the great literature of the state papers and the philosophers. The great teacher makes the blind see and the dumb speak but he can only do so because he too has had his tongue unstopped and his eyes opened.

The first and most important function of Liberal Arts education is to give amplitude and width to the human personality and to enable that personality to express itself fully, clearly, precisely, and gracefully. Style is a matter of ultimate importance whether one is writing up the minutes of the schoolboard or pitching soft-ball for one of the local leagues, and style can be learned.

The great Roman historian Tacitus in his *Dialogue on Oratory*, in which he discusses the change in oratory from Cicero's to his own day, implies that the decay of oratory was in fact due to the decline of republican institutions. It is the thesis of Tacitus that oratory could be great only in the push and shove of republican politics. Surely in Tacitus' day as in our own day there is a relationship between oratory and politics, between political vision and political utterance and the health of the Republic. Whatever may have been the case in the first century A.D., I think it most likely that political difficulties stem, at least in part, from the decay of oratory, the decay of the rhetorical tradition rather than the rhetorical tradition simply reflecting the decay of the constitution. It has been observed that one cannot now imagine the residents of Illinois' small towns turning out now for a political debate in the style of the Lincoln-Douglas debates. It is not simply that an audience would not attend or would be inattentive if they did attend. To a far greater extent candidates who are capable of debating the issues in a knowledgeable and trenchant manner are lacking. How often in the past two decades have you turned away from the televised presidential debates in embarrassed and stunned amazement. The decay of the rhetorical tradition has exacted a terrible price in our democratic society. Presidential speeches since Herbert Hoover have rarely been written by the President himself but rather are the productions of a team of ghosts who coax a set of political platitudes which long ago died of pernicious anemia into a temporary resurrection.

Our republican political institutions are based upon a widespread contact with a traditional political culture. The founding fathers were, as we all know, intimately acquainted with the masterpieces of political theory, ancient and modern. Ordinary men and women read such documents as the *Federalist Papers* with avidity and took part in the great political debates of their time. Permit me to drive home this picture of the past level of rhetorical education and interest in the United States with a quotation from Alexis de Tocqueville's *Democracy in America.* Tocqueville writes towards the end of Vol. I:

> . . . At the extreme borders of the confederated states, upon the confines of society and the wilderness, a population of bold adventurers have taken up their abode, who pierce the solitudes of the American woods to seek a country there in order to escape the poverty that awaited them in their native home. As soon as the pioneer reaches the place which is to serve him for a retreat, he fells a few trees and builds a loghouse. Nothing can offer a more miserable aspect than these isolated dwellings. The traveler who approaches one of them towards nightfall sees the flicker of the hearth flame through the chinks in the walls; and at night, if the wind rises, he hears the roof of boughs shake to and fro in the midst of the great forest trees. Who would not suppose that this poor hut is the asylum of rudeness and ignorance? Yet no sort of comparison can be drawn between the pioneer and the dwelling that shelters him. Everything about him is primitive and wild, but he is himself the result of the labor and experience of eighteen centuries. He wears the dress and speaks the language of cities; he is acquainted with the past, curious about the future, and ready for argument about the present; he is, in short, a highly civilized being, who consents for a time to inhabit the backwoods, and who

penetrates into the wilds of the New World with the Bible, an axe, and some newspapers. It is difficult to imagine the incredible rapidity with which thought circulates in these deserts. I do not think that so much intellectual activity exists in the most enlightened and populous districts of France.[3]

On the occasion of the bicentennial of American Independence Irving Kristol in a lecture observed:

> . . . It is we, their political descendants, who tend to be unaware of the novelty of the American political enterprise, and of the risks and ambiguity inherent in that novelty. We simplify and vulgarize and distort, because we have lost the sense of how bold and innovative the Founding Fathers were, and of how problematic — necessarily problematic — is the system of government, and the society, which they established. Witness the fact that, incredibly enough, at our major universities it is almost impossible to find a course, graduate or undergraduate, devoted to *The Federalist*.[4]

The continued survival and vigor of American political institutions is dependent upon the transmission of America's political tradition, the inculcation of a deep political culture. It is not enough to know the mechanics of government and the political slogans of the moment. Americans must be acquainted with all that Rhetoric taught and implied in the liberal arts tradition.

But even a revival of the rhetorical tradition will not be enough to preserve us as a functioning republic. It is often forgotten because of the pluralistic nature of our society how dependent we are upon a very large measure of consensus to make our society functional. The great crisis of the Civil War and the disorders of the 1960's and early 1970's drove home the fact that our society necessarily is more accurately characterized by consensus than pluralism and that when divisions become too deep our political institutions cease to function well or function not at all.

It seems to me that one of the chief functions of Liberal Arts education is to expose those broad areas of agreement in values, in attitudes, in culture and political behavior which are the *sine qua non* without which we cannot have an ordered society.

By this I do not mean that Liberal Arts education is nothing more than indoctrination and inculcation. Our system is based upon the agreement of rational men. They have arrived at that agreement through debate and discussion. They have arrived at that agreement through a study of the best the past has to offer by way of theory and of deed. They have arrived at that agreement by an analysis of present difficulties and possibilities. No small part of consensus is based upon a knowledge of the limits of pluralism; an assessment of the centrality of any value or position to the survival of the common life. Much of the tragedy of politics in our recent past derived from the fact that men acted out of ignorance of common values and the assumption that the unexamined opinions of the individual were the only valid tests of political validity and justice. In 1981 the most practical study in the world, a study upon which our survival depends, is the study of those things, values, culture and politics which make us "one out of many" and which provide a common life in the midst of pluralism. This is one of the greatest functions of the Liberal Arts tradition in our society.

It is often argued that the Liberal Arts are fine for leisure-time pursuits but that in the work-a-day world of America in 1981 what we need and want is vocational training, preparation for the role the student will occupy in the world of work. No one denies the necessity to earn a living and to fulfill a useful function in the world. No one, I hope, will reject the notion that we are most free when we commit ourselves to service. This implies, of course, that we know why we serve and that we know what we serve and that knowledge alone reaches well beyond the confines of a narrow technical training. No doubt all education is in some ultimate sense, vocational.

One of the most threatening aspects of present-day society is the profound sense of alienation which pervades the work place. For most workers, regardless of the task or social role which they labor to fulfill the only force which keeps them at their task is the wage they receive. Making and doing has ceased in the eyes of the maker and doer to be intrinsically valuable and a source of joy and pleasure. The reason that this is the case is that the attainment of technical skill has been cut off from rational purpose.

I am not so silly as to propose that Liberal Arts education is going to eliminate alienated labor and yet I do believe that any education which places labor, no matter how routine and humble in the context of the larger scheme of things makes labor more valuable and important to the person who performs it and, in a very important respect, liberates the individual. To be bound to a task whose purpose one does not comprehend and whose value one does not understand is servile no matter that the chains which bind one to it are made of money rather than of iron.

The full consequences of alienated labor were clearly grasped by the great German historian, Friedrich Meinecke, who after World War II looked back over his own long lifetime and recent German history and attempted to find an explanation for what he called the "German Catastrophe." Meinecke wrote:

> . . . Technology's expansion into all walks of practical life in general called into existence a great number of new crafts and careers. It thereby finally created a new social class whose psychological structure is markedly different from that of previous social classes, both those of the old agrarian state and those of the new bourgeoisie which has blossomed out of the agrarian state. An intellect sharply concentrated upon whatever was utilitarian and immediately serviceable took possession of mental life. Through it great things could be achieved, resulting in an astonishing progress in civilization. Man's other spiritual forces, so far as they were not suppressed, avenged themselves either by those wild reactions just mentioned or fell into general decay and debility. Feeling and phantasy, as it were, had the choice between running wild or withering. Generally they did the latter. The craving of the senses, indestructible as it is and always will be in man, received as a result of the progress of technology and civilization an abundance of new objects towards which it could direct itself. The will, as a result of the fabulous possibilities now being made attainable in practical life through the calculating and planning intellect, received a powerful stimulus and upsurge. Indeed, the later nineteenth and twentieth centuries have not been lacking in tremendous energies. The calculating intellect aimed more at practical

activities than at spiritual understanding. It combined with a concentrated will power, stormed from one ostensible tremendous task to another, and only paused momentarily for relief in the material pleasures of life. Such in general outline is the picture offered by the genius of the century, a very different picture from that of the decaying late Roman Empire with which people have often compared our era.[5]

Technology divorced from a rational and human context is the great danger to our era and to our society. Ultimately it will fail because it does not fulfill the human life but before that absolute failure it can and has done terrible damage. In every area of human endeavor men today face questions of ultimate, that is, life and death consequences, questions engendered by the possibilities which their technologies present to them. Technological skill and expertise will not answer these questions nor can they be evaded. We can pretend that these questions do not exist. We can confidently assert that if anything is technologically possible, that alone is a warrant for making it a reality. The consequence of such a line of action is the eventuation of an ugly and irresponsible world of mean and petty gratifications purchased at the cost of an unsuspecting mankind and the agony of future generations.

Max Weber, the great German sociologist, at the very end of his book, *The Protestant Ethic and the Spirit of Capitalism*, depicted what the consequences of such an unfettered technological order might be like when he wrote:

> No one knows who will live in this [iron] cage in the future, or whether at the end of this tremendous development entirely new prophets will arise, or there will be a great rebirth of old ideas and ideals, or, if neither, mechanized petrification, embellished with a sort of convulsive self-importance. For the last stage of this cultural development, it might be truly said: "Specialists without spirit, sensualists without heart; this nullity imagines that it has attained a level of civilization never before achieved."[6]

Before this final stage is reached, it is likely in my estimation that technological skill itself will have failed; the hand will have lost its cunning, the mind its capacity for narrow calculation. Ultimately, technological training is dependent upon a belief in the ultimate validity of all making and doing. When the religious, humanistic, rationalist context of technology is entirely lost technology itself will have passed beyond the unwilling reach of mankind. The truth is that we can have the achievements of technology only so long as we will and wish beyond technology.

The choice in education is not a choice between the liberal arts and a more narrow and exclusively technical training. All good education is vocational education but it must be vocational in the broadest sense and it must serve the needs of the whole man and not simply the diminished simulacrum of what it means to be fully human. Skills are as necessary as values. In the ideal educational system they are complementary rather than exclusive. It is the task of the teacher to demonstrate the relationship between the practical and the mundane, and the eternal; to show how the material goods are related to the "common good" and that good which is ultimate and absolute.

NOTES

1. William James, "The Sentiment of Rationality," in *Selected Papers on Philosophy* (London: J.M. Dent & Sons, 1917), p. 153.
2. Czeslaw Milosz, "Readings" in *Bells in Winter*, translated by the author and Lillian Vallee (New York: Ecco Press, 1980), p. 10.
3. Alexis de Tocqueville, *Democracy in America*. The Henry Reeve text as revised by Francis Bowen now further corrected and edited with introduction, editorial notes, and bibliographies by Phillips Bradley (New York: Alfred A. Knopf, 1966), Vol. I, pp. 316-317.
4. Irving Kristol, "The American Revolution as a Successful Revolution" in *America's Continuing Revolution, An Act of Conservation*, introduction by S. J. Tonsor (American Enterprise Institute for Public Policy Research, Washington, D.C., 1975), p. 20.

5. Friedrich Meinecke, *The German Catastrophe, Reflections and Recollections*, translated by Sidney B. Fay (Cambridge, Mass.: Harvard University Press, 1950).
6. Max Weber, *The Protestant Ethic and the Spirit of Capitalism*, translated by Talcott Parsons (New York: Charles Scribner's Sons, 1958), p. 182.

Chapter 3

General Education in a Free Society

SIDNEY HOOK

By "general education" I mean a course of study in the arts and sciences which may legitimately be required of students in institutions of liberal learning at the post-secondary school level. It is a course of study that usually precedes specialization or education for a vocation or calling but may accompany it.

Under the influence of Columbia College and then Harvard College, this conception of general education became a paradigm in the second quarter of our century for the curricula of most American liberal arts colleges that prided themselves upon their aspirations for educational excellence. This paradigm was shattered during the student revolutions of the sixties when, against the background of vandalized buildings and occupied administrative offices, faculties yielded to the demands of students that their course of study be "relevant" to the social and political concerns of American society as the students saw it. Actually, the students' revolt was not fired in the least — certainly not initially —by dissatisfaction with the educational experience. The student leaders on campuses from Berkeley to Cambridge, in response to surveys seeking to uncover the causes of their discontent, never listed the curricular fare on which they had been brought up as proximate or even remote influences. They did list a number of grave issues that agitated them — of war and peace, of poverty and social injustice, of racial discrimination and environmental pollution, for whose existence colleges and universities had not the slightest responsibility, issues whose resolution was beyond the competence and power of educational institutions to settle, and which in a political democracy were the business not of elites or hastily mobilized masses of students to resolve but of the citizenry as a whole.

Unable immediately to effect changes in national policy in these areas, the students discovered that they were extremely powerful on their own turf. They could not affect Congress or other governmental agencies but they could have their way with respect to the curriculum. Educational democracy, they cried, meant not only participation in the learning process but the freedom to decide what to learn, when, and even how to be judged on one's achievements. The consequence was a wholesale abolition of course requirements abetted in many institutions by a compliant and intimidated faculty unable or unwilling to defend general education. The curricular revolution as a rule was welcomed by administrators in the prayerful hope that this would slake the revolutionary thirst of students and contain the area of their disruption. The result was inescapable. With the fragmentation of general education it was possible in most institutions for students to complete their college studies and earn a degree without submitting themselves to the discipline of important areas of knowledge and experience. A potpourri of courses took the place of a coherently organized curriculum. One could not presuppose that students were familiar with the history of their own culture or acquainted with the great milestones in literature, science or art. Today we are witnessing a pendular swing back to the concept of a structured curriculum of general education, spurred by complex motivations and causes, but I have seen no evidence that a coherent educational philosophy is at work in the present-day reconstruction of general education. In the absence of such a philosophy, the curricula designed to meet passing needs and moods are not likely to be found justifiable when challenged.

I do not want to be misunderstood. I am not saying that the

existence of a philosophically justifiable curriculum of general education would have withstood, and that in the future they will withstand, the nihilistic attacks of enraged students. Unable to use the campus as a sanctuary for their forays against the society which nurtured them, these student crusaders for a better life in a better society were prepared to bring the walls of the academy tumbling around them regardless of the curriculum. Few colleges during the period of the so-called student revolution, regardless of the character of the curriculum, were able to emerge unscathed. Even Catholic colleges with required curricula (although they could hardly pass muster as genuine liberal arts institutions) were victimized with the odd result that some Jesuit institutions dropped the study of the philosophy of Thomas Aquinas as a requirement. The character of a society is determined not by its schools alone but by a whole complex of other institutions. The effects of formal education or schooling on social change are indirect. Who would have anticipated that Hitler and National Socialism would triumph in a nation whose classical and modern gymnasia provided a rigorous and required curriculum that exceeded the demands of most American liberal arts colleges on their students?

One of the things that impressed me most during "the time of troubles" of American higher education was the failure of American faculty spokesmen to offer a rational defense of general education against student criticisms, especially of its requirements, and of the deprivation of the students' freedom to choose whatever courses they wished to complete their education. Indeed, most faculty members were unable to justify requirement of the study of their own disciplines, no less the requirement of the disciplines of their colleagues. On several crucial occasions during faculty deliberations on what studies should be required of students matriculating for a liberal arts degree, I have heard spokesmen for some disciplines argue that unless their subjects were required, a considerable number of their colleagues would have to be declared in excess and face the prospect of unemployment. As if this had the slightest bearing on the central question!

In order to focus and dramatize the challenge, I am going to repeat the words addressed to my colleagues by a highly articulate student rebel leader at a faculty meeting of the

Washington Square College of New York University:

> "After all," she said, "the intrinsic value or interest of a subject isn't enough to justify prescribing it. For every subject has intrinsic value but not to everybody, and judging by the behavior and attitude of some of our teachers, not even to those who make their living teaching it to us. If education is to be effective and relevant to the lives of students, it must be related to the personal and individual needs of the students. Without *us*, there is no role for you as teachers."

And then turning to me, who was then the acting spokesman of the curriculum committee, she let fly this barbed question: "Who are *you*, or anyone else, to tell *me* what my educational needs are? I, and I alone, am the best judge of what I want and what I need. And what is true for me is true for everyone. That's what I understand by democracy in education."

Were that student present at this conference, she might have phrased her challenge to us as follows: "Since your premise is that freedoms are indivisible, how can you justify a program of general education that proscribes my educational freedom to study what I please?"

I shall not try to answer this last question because I do *not* believe that all freedoms are indivisible. On the contrary, I believe that historically and analytically the statement about the indivisibility of freedom is questionable. Since no freedom is absolute, there is a point at which it must be limited in order to safeguard other desirable freedoms. Historically, the American Revolution sounded the tocsin for political freedom, but was carried out by men who approved of and practiced slavery at the time.

But I shall try to defend the philosophy behind general education by an extended response to the first series of questions. To begin with, I shall readily concede that students are or should be free to determine whether or not they wish to continue their post-secondary schooling, and if they do, they should be free to determine whether or not they wish to study at large or small, metropolitan or rural, unisex or coeducational institutions, and finally, after they have completed the requirements of a general education, they should be free to choose their areas of specialization or professional orientation. That is the limit of their educational freedom. Beyond that it is the educator's task to determine what areas of knowledge and skills may reasonably be required of students, and what the level of proficiency is to be attained therein, before they receive the certificate or diploma or the judgment of educational adequacy.

I am particularly concerned to contest the assertion that because a student knows what he or she *wants*, he knows what he or she *needs* educationally, and is necessarily the best judge of it. Very few students can justifiably claim that they are equipped to know what their medical needs are. To determine them some medical knowledge is necessary. It is no different as a rule with the student's educational needs. I am assuming, of course, competent and sympathetic advisors who are concerned with the student's history and background.

We should acknowledge that any prescribed curriculum should be designed to meet the student's educational needs, and to defend the basic outlines of the curriculum in a rational interchange with any student interested. I shall very hastily sketch the way in which we can establish a desirable general education program not by imposing it in virtue of adult authority, but by appealing to the verifiable individual needs of students. In doing so, I shall follow the suggestions of John Dewey who maintained that there are three basic considerations that should enter into the development of the curriculum on any level: (1) the nature and needs of the student; (2) the nature and needs of the society in which students live; and (3) subject matters whose study is required to further their intellectual and emotional growth. And it may surprise this audience that the scheme of general education I derived from these considerations many years ago, and which was exemplified for a short time in the Unified Studies Program of Washington Square College, New York University, received John Dewey's endorsement. Here is a thumbnail sketch of the areas of study, not the detailed courses, that may vary from time to time and from institution to institution, and their justifications for inclusion in the curricular substance of general education.

1. "Every student has an objective need to be able to communicate clearly and effectively with his fellow men (or women), to grasp with comprehension and accuracy different types of discourse he or she will encounter in their ordinary

experience, and to express his or her thought and emotion in a literate way at least in his or her native tongue.

2. "Every student needs to have at least some rudimentary knowledge about his or her own body and mind, about the world of nature and its determining forces, about evolution and genetics, and allied matters that are central to a rational belief about the place of man in the universe. If students are to have any understanding of these things, they must have more than miscellaneous information about isolated facts. They must have some grasp of the principles that explain what they observe, and some conception of the nature of scientific method. It is a commonplace that the modern world is what it is largely in virtue of the impact of science and technology on nature and society. No one can feel at home in the world today ignorant of science. More and more career opportunities presuppose some familiarity with scientific application. The future may require the use of computers on the same scale as the present-day use of typewriters.

3. "All students have a need to become intelligently aware of how their society functions, its past and its traditions, of the great historical, economic and social forces shaping its future, of the alternatives of development still open, of the problems, threats, promises and predicaments they and their fellow citizens must face. Whether students want to revolutionize society or save it from revolution, they must acquire a historical perspective without which old evils may reappear under new faces and labels. Those who act as if they were born yesterday and imagine they can escape history and build from scratch are dangerous simplifiers. They mistake their own impatience and audacity as evidence for the objective readiness of things, and often wreck the lives of others in the wreckage of their vain and ignorant hopes.

4. "All students need to be informed, not only of significant facts and theories about nature, society and the human psyche but also of the conflict of values and ideals in our time, of the great maps of life under which human beings are enrolled. Because no important policy is ever a purely technical question, students must learn how to uncover the

inescapable value judgments behind proposed policies, and to relate them to their causes and consequences, and to their costs in other values.

5. "All students need to acquire some methodological sophistication that should sharpen their sense of evidence, relevance and canons of valid inference. They should be able to distinguish between disguised definitions or *a priori* assumptions and genuine empirical statements, between resolutions and generalizations. In popular discourse and debate they should be able to nail the obvious statistical lie, to detect the systematic bias in so much of our public media, and to acquire an emotional as well as intellectual immunity to rhetorical claptrap.

6. "Finally, all students have a need — perhaps it would not be too strong to say that they have an educational right — to be introduced to the cultural legacies of their civilization, its art, literature and music. Critical method should be central to all learning in general education as a permanent antidote to gullibility but it need not lead to the death or atrophy of the imagination. The arts, literary, dramatic, poetic and other multiple forms, should be cultivated not only because they develop the sensibilities and provide an unfailing occasion of delight and enjoyment in the present but also because they are a permanent source of enrichment of experience in the future. They not only make possible the creative use of leisure but help in the emergence of that inner landscape without which one cannot live in serenity during times when one must stand alone."

These needs, I submit, define the required areas of study of general education — areas of study, I repeat, not specific courses. Once we agree on this as the common minimum indispensables of study in the foundational years of higher education, a multiplicity of problems remains to be solved, most of them of detail, e.g., how much of mathematics should be required and in what context, how broad the history, what level of science, what works of literature, what foreign language, if any, etc.

I pass these questions by to address myself to some of the larger issues. What is the relation between this scheme of general education and the concepts of freedom and a free society? These are very large and complex concepts and I do not propose a comprehensive analysis of all of their facets. By a free or open society I mean one whose institutions rest upon direct or indirect processes of uncoerced consent. It is a society in which there is freedom for its citizens to choose the religion they profess, the economic system under which they wish to live, the degree of government intervention and control they are willing to accept, and, of course, their political rulers. A free society in short is a democratic society in which minority rights are protected and respected by the majority.

What has general education to do with all this? First, the kind of general education I have described is one pervaded by a spirit of critical inquiry in which all things may be doubted and where conclusions rest upon evidence and argument. Such an education can flourish only in a democratic society. I know of no educational system of general education in the past, whether in ancient or medieval times, that did not set up roadblocks to inquiry concerning some sacred dogmas of faith and belief. Second, properly implemented general education prepares citizens to exercise their duties as citizens with greater knowledge and responsibility. It exposes them to the central disciplines, encourages them to achieve the full power of their thought, and leaves them to themselves to make the decisions and commitments of vocation and faith.

But surely, we are bound to hear some say: "This is not enough. If we wish to preserve our free society, our education must bend the twig to produce the appropriate flower. Its basic axioms must not be challenged or questioned but reinforced by all sorts of methods, rational to be sure but non-rational also, of winning assent." To which I reply: "I do not see the necessity of this kind of indoctrination if we are convinced that we have good reasons for our basic beliefs." Only persons of little faith in what they believe will seek to bar intellectual challenges to what they hold to be true. Those challenges will come anyhow from demagogues and pressure groups outside the walls of the academy. If so, why not consider them *inter muros*, as part of the curriculum, where they can be thoroughly dissected? The validity of democracy can be strengthened, not weakened, by an objective analysis of the theories of communism, fascism, or any other form of totalitarianism, especially when considered in the light of their practices.

In revulsion against the ritualistic liberalism of many university faculties and the raucous outcries of yesteryear, there is a tendency in some quarters to go from resistance to the politicalization of universities to a demand that universities espouse the *proper kind* of ideology. To safeguard students from subversion or from the demoralization that allegedly follows from subjecting traditional beliefs to the acids of critical analysis — as if reason could not cope with such challenges! It is sometimes urged that the university *as a corporate body*, commit itself institutionally to God, freedom, immortality, free enterprise or some other basic belief that seems threatened by the operations of free inquiry. Let us remember, however, that those who strove for the politicalization of the university during the stormy Sixties and Seventies were not carrying out the mandate of liberalism but betraying its principles as well as the guidelines of academic freedom painfully established by the professional associations of scholars in the twentieth century. The mission of the university has varied from medieval times to the present. It reflects the kind of society in which it is nurtured. In American democratic society, a consensus has been established on the goal or mission of the university. It is not the quest for salvation or power but the quest for significant truths in varied fields, their transmission and critical evaluation by teaching and publication, and the promotion of programs of study, research and teaching to further these ends. This is the primary objective. Although many other activities of the university are legitimate, none should be countenanced that violate this basic objective. It goes without saying, or should go without saying, that within the confines of academic freedom and integrity, members of the faculty, as distinct from the university as such, should be free to hold and profess whatever views they regard as valid. It is true, unfortunately, that in some disciplines in some institutions, there is a lack of balance, a one-sidedness and partiality in the presentation of controversial issues. This can sometimes be remedied by administrative leadership and public criticism by courageous scholars. It should not be the concern of any state agencies or the object of legislative action.

There remains the very large questions about the relation between general education, the nature of man, and the cosmos. There are some philosophers of education who maintain that without some metaphysical or theological underpinning, no satisfactory curriculum can be constructed. Some even think they can deduce the content of such a curriculum from antecedently held views about the nature of man, the nature of knowledge, and the nature of nature. Although I am open to argument and evidence for such a view, I believe it is profoundly mistaken, that the question about a desirable curriculum can be settled without reference to first or last things.

Consider that the curriculum of general education is to be devised for all students — regardless of their sex, race, national origin, religion or doctrinal beliefs. Is it at all plausible that we can establish theoretically or practically a community unified by a metaphysical or theological Weltanschauung that will give us curricular guidance? In this field, disagreements have existed since the beginning of recorded time, and there is no commonly recognized and accepted method of negotiating differences. Further, it is demonstrable that no curriculum can be uniquely derived from any metaphysical proposition whatsoever. Far more fruitful in building a desirable curriculum is to assess the fruits or consequences of alternative approaches in imparting the knowledge, developing the skills, and cultivating the values we deem appropriate for the education of modern men and women — and making our decision.

One concluding word based on the verifiable truth that students are more affected by their teachers than by the subject matters they are taught. Except in the areas of their specialization, students do not retain for long the details of instruction. But they have vivid recollections of the teachers in any field who have opened new vistas or infect them with an enthusiasm for a new interest or taught them how to see, listen and think in ways until then unfamiliar to them. The promise of the curriculum of general education can best be realized if it is taught by a corps of gifted teachers who are willing and able to cooperate in what is an interdisciplinary enterprise. In the past, where general education curriculums have failed, they have been killed by boredom, generated by young, inexperienced and callow instructors who have been assigned to their task as a chore by their seniors. It is notorious that the worst teaching in modern American education takes place on the tertiary or college level where the age-old illusion flourishes that anyone who really knows a subject matter knows how to teach it. The faculty of general education should be drawn from those scholars who are aware that teaching is an art whose practice, as in all arts, can be improved. But this is a theme for another day.

Chapter 4

The University and the Universe

STANLEY L. JAKI

I am convinced I can speak in the name of all present, bene-
ficiaries of a provident Alma Mater, which in her generosity
imposes upon us only one obligation, the pleasant duty of
exchanging ideas across the universal field of knowledge. Ours
is a state of sweet do-nothing, a sort of *dolce far niente;* no
courses, no exams, no papers to correct. Our sole business is
learning for learning's sake. Two famous educators, were they
here with us, would point out that such a gathering has an
uncanny likeness to what they held to be the ideal of a
university. John Henry Newman, as you all know, held high the
view that the university is an institution which "merely brought
a number of young men together for three or four years and
then sent them away." He contrasted it with that organization
which "gave its degrees to any person who passed an examination in a wide range of subjects." The contrast was also
between an institution which to all appearances "did nothing"
except insist on residence of students and tutors, and an
organization "which exacted of its members an acquaintance
with every science under the sun."[1] The other educator, Mark
Hopkins, president of Williams College and a contemporary of
Newman, went about his business with an informality and

naturalness which evoked the best in the American character and prompted James Garfield, a Williams alumnus, to his famed remark: "The university is a student on one end of a pine log and Mark Hopkins on the other."[2]

In this graphic picture of a student and a teacher doing in all appearance nothing but shooting the breeze, Newman would, in spite of all his love of the ancient formalities of Oxford, recognize his ideal of the university. He would be horrified at seeing the almost complete triumph of the concept of the university "as a factory of knowledge," a concept urged by T. H. Huxley,[3] a contemporary of both Newman and Hopkins. In such a factory he would easily recognize that modern version of universities which produce "numerates" instead of "literates"[4] and in which information passes from the mouth of the teacher to the ears of the student without having passed through the minds of either of them. It should be easy to guess Newman's reaction to universities in which a dissertation on time and motion comparison of four methods of dishwashing qualifies its author to the dignity of master of arts.[5] Churchill, who once spoke of "some chicken, some neck," might now say, "some masters, some arts." Newman would undoubtedly relish the concluding part of the remark according to which "Harvard offers education *a la carte*, Yale a substantial *table d'hote*, Columbia a quick lunch, and Princeton a picnic."[6] A picnic has something leisurely in it, almost invariably it includes the presence of one or more logs and above all the atmosphere in which thoughts flow unencumbered. Newman would of course shake his head in disbelief on hearing that some universities became, to quote a Chinese student visiting in the United States, "athletic institutions in which a few classes are held for the feeble-minded."[7] One can easily imagine Newman's revulsion to universities which turned into a grim game of musical chairs: students claiming to themselves the role of teaching, teachers wanting to administer, and the administration lamely footing the bill for the self-destructive tragicomedy. Newman would see tragedy loom large in a university which has for its switchboard rule that an outside or inside caller must give the number of a student, not his or her name. The university was for Newman an Alma Mater, "knowing her children one by one, not a foundry, or a mint, or a treadmill,"[8] or a computer printout, he would add, were he alive today. Great lover of books though he was, he would be dismayed by the phrase, old yet applicable in some places today, that a "true University of these days is a Collection of Books."[9] He would find revolting the spectre of universities eager "to make young men as unlike their fathers as possible."[10] Mindful of the old truth that the new morality is the old immorality, he would not be overly shocked on finding universities that "are fit for nothing but to debauch the principles of young men [and women]."[11] But nothing would shock him so much as the abdication of the search for meaning when voiced by spokesmen of illustrious universities, whether its presidents or eminent professors, especially when they do it in the name of knowledge.

Certainly, Newman was not an enemy of knowledge. Apart from his universally acknowledged scholarship, his idea of the university most explicitly contained a search for all knowledge, for knowledge in its universality. But precisely because he believed in the universality of knowledge, he held that knowledge was pursued for the sake of meaning, and above all for the sake of that most universal meaning which is God, the ultimate in intelligibility and being. This is why he made it the core of his idea of university that a university retain its *raison d'etre* only if philosophical or natural theology was the basis of its program of instruction.[12] Newman also knew that search for meaning was best done when the mind was free to reflect on and share in all kinds of knowledge, not only free in a political sense, but also free of psychological and social coercion. This is why he esteemed so highly the unstructured encounters between students and tutors, this is why he would have recognized his idea of a university in a pine log reserved for one student and one teacher. It is in such encounters that one asks the questions: What is the point of knowing or is knowledge ultimately pointless?

Most present-day universities, and especially the most prestigious ones, have, to all appearances, given up the search for meaning. Illustrations of this are the sundry utterances of especially two groups of scholars in great modern universities, cosmologists and biologists. They tower above their colleagues not so much because they have at their disposal dazzling equipment and control budgets vastly superior to those allotted other departments. Their superiority does not even rest on the all-inclusive and fundamental character of their empirical subject-matter: galaxies and genes. Their commanding role rather lies in the fact that they have somehow expropriated to themselves an authoritative role to think about universe and man. Of course, modern cosmologists (or fundamental particle physicists — their fields more and more overlap) and modern geneticists must think more than ever. From Einstein to Hawking, modern cosmology has been above all a feat of incisive thinking which almost invariably was a step or two ahead of observations. Genes had for long been a conceptual postulate before they were actually isolated, analysed and manipulated. Even today — when gene splicing is turning into a big industry and when leading universities are eager to secure millions from genetic discoveries made in their laboratories — it is well to recall that not so old story of the double helix. The story was more the story of a race among minds than of a race among laboratories.

Scientific thinking certainly deserves the highest admiration, but here too, as elsewhere, admiration can be easily misplaced. What is all too often forgotten about scientific thinking is that it is primarily thinking and only secondarily scientific. Even the most trivial scientific statement is steeped in philosophy, and to be blunt, steeped in plain metaphysics. The amount of metaphysics in scientific statements increases in the measure in which these statements become more inclusive. At the point where these statements become valuational, their tie to truth will not be scientific at all but thoroughly philosophical or metaphysical. First-rate scientists should therefore provoke not admiration but consternation when after frowning at length on philosophy they wax utterly philosophical. A case in point is the concluding remark in S. Weinberg's masterly popularization of modern cosmology, *The First Three Minutes:* "The more the universe seems comprehensible, the more it also seems pointless."[13] A more concise and telling illustration of the ultimate tragicomedy which is the hallowed atmosphere of great modern universities, could hardly be found. Unlike some cosmologists, who today celebrate the lack of comprehension, biologists have for more than a hundred years revelled in equally crude philosophical non-sequiturs. In particular I mean their purposeful debunking of purpose. They not only get away with it, but earn interminable applause for the farce.

One example, and a fairly recent one, the reception of Prof. E. O. Wilson's book, *On Human Nature*, should suffice. Although it comes to a close with the admission that "the mythology of scientific materialism" is both liberating and enslaving through its ultimate offering which is "blind hope," the book earned accolades for its philosophical merits. A book which proclaims in the same breath both liberation and enslavement should have appeared suspect prima facie, but not in this age of modal logic. Only the old fashioned disjunctive logic entitles one to ask that if man, as Prof. Wilson insisted, was merely a system to secure the survival of viable genes,[14] where was his liberation? Is it not a cruel joke to cheer up a prisoner, never to be released from jail, by telling him that he should feel liberated through being informed about his unchangeable imprisonment? Again, was it not rudely farcical on the part of Professor Wilson, praised by another reviewer as "a thoughtful scientist,"[15] to claim that *On Human Nature* was "the third book in a trilogy that unfolded without my being consciously aware of the logical sequence until it was nearly finished?"[16] No readable book, not even the opium-eater Coleridge's *Enchanted Forest* and *Road to Xanadu*, was ever written without its author having a conscious advance view of its plan and message.[17] What makes *On Human Nature* not only a very readable, but also a very coherent and instructive book is, in fact, the very force of premises to which Prof. Wilson is consciously captive throughout the book.

That the last pages of the book should ring of despair, should seem a foregone conclusion to anyone ready to pause over the startling motto of the book, a quotation from David Hume. This was perhaps not clearly foreseen by Prof. Wilson. But it is testimony to his greatness as a thinker (his greatness as a scientist does not need my praises) that he stuck to his premises through thick and thin, even at the price of ending with the patently contradictory message of simultaneous liberation and enslavement. Perhaps he could not simply extricate himself from the hold of system-making, the lure of which is much stronger than generally suspected. At any rate, Prof. Wilson's contradictory message and his claim that purpose can nowhere be seen, should seem farcical even on a cursory look. The fact is, however, that most academic faces turn rather sour when reminded of Whitehead's famous remark, made half a century ago, that scientists who devote themselves to the purpose of proving that there is no purpose, constitute an interesting subject for study.[18] The tragicomedy is indeed complete. In modern universities, all too often equipped with plush theaters, faculty weep over their performance when they should laugh, and smile when they should hang their heads in shame.

The immediate cause of their shame should be their playing a facile game with philosophy. They do not seem to have taken for more than an artful fishing for compliments the dictum of Einstein, a most eminent among scientists, that "the man of science is a poor philosopher."[19] Quite possibly Einstein himself did not realize what a poor philosopher he was. He could never articulate that realism and its meaningfulness to which he was driven by his scientific creativity.[20] To the end he made relapses either into Kantian idealism or Machist sensationism, the two philosophies which he imbibed as a youth, and both of which he disowned once he perceived the true meaning of his work in physics. As all too often in the past, in our century too, it remained to others, usually philosophers, to articulate the deeds and words of leading scientists, and to unveil, if necessary, the tragicomedy lurking behind some of their utterances. Such a role on the part of the philosophers should not seem to be surprising as most of the time scientists speak of two heavily philosophical subjects, man and the universe. Both are vast topics even for a series of lectures, and are also very different topics. Yet they have one very important trait in common: both man and universe are invisible to physical eyes. That we cannot take a physical look at the universe because we, being a part of it, cannot get outside it, should be obvious. As to man, I do not wish to rekindle old debates about universals of which man, Socrates, was the chief whipping boy. To those who dismiss that debate as a scholastic play with words, let me recall a story about Claude Bernard, certainly not a scholastic and not even a philosopher by profession. When asked whether the study of life demanded a mechanistic or a vitalistic philosophy, he curtly replied: "I have never seen life,"[21] with physical eyes, of course.

The phenomenon of mere organic life lands us deep into metaphysics. And so does the universe.

This last remark should seem particularly appropriate in this year of 1981, the 200th anniversary of the publication of Kant's *Critique of Pure Reason*. If there is a book of which cosmologists should be wary, it is the *Critique*. The same holds true for all scientists, if it is true, and it certainly is, that all science is cosmology.[22] For if the *Critique* is right, cosmologists and all scientists can only be wrong, and should consider themselves to be the victims of a tragic illusion. For a chief aim of the *Critique* is that the notion of cosmos, or universe, is not a valid notion; in fact, to recall Kant's claim, the notion of the universe is merely the bastard product of the metaphysical cravings of the intellect.[23] Actually, it is Kant's procedure to validate this claim that should seem both dastardly and clever at the same time. The cleverness relates to the fact that he first took on the universe and only afterwards man. The cosmological antinomies precede the anthropological ones. Once the validity of the cosmos is undermined, it is far easier to lock man within himself and secure for him thereby an absolute autonomy, the ultimate aim of the *Critique,* though a much earlier aim of its author.[24] The dastardliness of the antinomies as articulated by Kant is glaring. He shifted grounds from idealism to empiricism, choosing now the one, now the other, to suit his immediate strategy which aimed at enveloping both universe and man in a fog of uncertainty. As to the universe, idealism provided his argument that the universe could not be demonstrably finite, and he fell back on empiricism to support the opposite, namely, the impossibility of proving the infinity of the universe. A universe which thus appeared to be without contours was for Kant an entity which man tried in vain to grasp, let alone to use it as a stepping stone to the ultimate of being and intelligibility, usually referred to as God.

Were Kant alive today, he would be tormented by the fact that the very same science, which he took for his stronghold, though he knew very little about it,[25] achieved rigorous ways to deal with the totality of consistently interacting things, the universe. In this century of science explosion, we are often overawed by our ability to explode the atom and far less impressed by a much more explosive scientific achievement, the formulation for the first time in history, of a genuinely scientific cosmology. The success in that latter respect is far from being complete. Things interact in more than one way, not only gravitationally but also electromagnetically. There are in addition the nuclear forces binding the nucleus, and the force binding the quarks, the constituent part of nucleons (protons and neutrons), a force which is the subject of the so-called chromodynamics. The formulation of a Unified Theory in which all these forces, and perhaps some others, will be seen as the manifestation of one single force or interaction, is the great aim of leading scientists today. A chief reason of their confidence relates to Einstein's General Theory of Relativity. In General Relativity scientific cosmology found its true birth insofar as the theory gives a paradox-free account of all material bodies which consistently interact with one another gravitationally.

The magnitude of Einstein's achievement can only be perceived when set against a rather dark background. It consists of the insensitivity which scientists displayed throughout the 18th and 19th centuries toward the gravitational and optical paradoxes of an infinite Euclidean homogenous universe of stars. The paradoxes were sufficiently stringent to suggest the impossibility of such a universe. To my knowledge, only two scientists, Zöllner in Leipzig and Clifford in London, did recognize in full, around 1870, that a lecture of Riemann, given in 1854, provided the possibility of a paradox-free, that is, contradiction-free cosmology.[26] The name of Riemann should evoke non-Euclidean geometry and a four-dimensional space-time manifold. Indeed, Einstein's General Relativity, or at least its cosmological chapter, was not without some anticipations, none of which made a real stir.[27] The idea of an infinite Euclidean universe so strongly dominated the thinking of scientists around 1900 as to make them adopt a schizophrenic state of mind. They took the Milky Way for an all-inclusive entity. While they believed that stars and galaxies stretched to infinity, they conveniently wrote off everything beyond the Milky Way as irrelevant for science.

Beneath this infatuation with Euclidean infinity there lay considerations that were inspired by Plotinos' pantheism. This is not to suggest that Pseudo-Dionysius, a still-elusive Eighth-century author, wanted to graft pantheism on Christian thought as he propagated the notion of God's infinity in a distinctly emanationist or Plotinist sense.[28] He took God's infinity in a positive sense, in a distinct departure from Christian tradition, for which the term is negative, a tradition which on this point too was emphatically voiced by Thomas Aquinas. During the centuries of decaying Scholasticism less and less attention was given to the dangers implied in the notion of infinity. Even in the case of Cusanus, piety and scientific acumen were not enough to keep those dangers in focus. Distrustful of philosophy, Cusanus declared under distinctly Plotinist influences that the creation must be similar to the Creator. With some strict reservations the declaration can still be Christian; with no such reservations it opens the floodgates first to pantheism and then to strict materialism in which the infinite universe unashamedly plays the role of God. Indeed, a Giordano Bruno, a champion of pantheism, is Cusanus without Christian faith and piety. The parallels among the dicta of the two are legion, or rather Bruno plagiarized Cusanus to an astonishing degree. One illustration of these parallels should suffice. Cusanus did his best to eliminate the distinction between planets and stars. With great vehemence Bruno did the same. Indeed the chief characteristic of the universe, both in Cusanus' and in Bruno's version is that it tends to lose its clear distinct specific features.[29] The presence of Plotinist theology in Newton's cosmology, a further major step in the story, is best seen in Newton's insistence on the infinity of space as sensorium of an infinite God. Kant, that is the young Kant, author of a cosmological work, merely echoed an all too common theme of his time, when he spiritedly argued that only an infinite creation is worthy of an infinite god.[30] Before long, Kant needed no God, or even a universe, for that matter.

A chief difficulty which plagued Newtonian physics was the material entity, the ether which filled infinite space. The ether, as is well known, could not be given paradox-free properties. At this point nothing would be more tempting than to jump to Einstein. Is not he, in all cliché accounts, the glorious St. George who beheaded that dragon, the science of the ether? The cliché is certainly effective in drawing attention away from a crucial chapter in that theological story about infinity. In that crucial chapter many 19th-century agnostics and materialists would have room, but none so prominently as Herbert Spencer. Spencerian philosophy is an elaborate materialist theology of an infinite universe.[31] The chief characteristic of that theology is an effortless flow of words in which the emergence of the specific from the non-specific, the differentiated from the undifferentiated, is being set forth. Herbert Spencer is the 19th-century Giordano Bruno who in a discourse, which contains nothing of Bruno's crudities and which, unlike Bruno's discourse, has all the semblance of science, dissolves the specificities of the universe into an endless sea of non-specificities. Herbert Spencer, it is well to recall, was a foremost champion of the nebular hypothesis, or Kant-Laplace theory, the starting point of which is a nebula which, as far as science was concerned, was nebulosity itself,[32] that is, the absence of all specificity. Reference to Spencer and specificity should remind one of Darwin, whose message was far more than the plea on behalf of the emergence of a species from another. The closeness of the word species to specificity is in itself suggestive of another far deeper issue. It is the story of the instinctive struggle of materialists (Darwin was an avowed one from the start)[33] against cosmic specificity. The cosmological dicta of Marx, Engels, and Lenin, tell the same story.[34]

Chronologically, we are now at the turn of the century when scientists, both believers and non-believers, firmly asserted the infinity of the universe, on spurious theological or countertheological grounds, and, in one way or another, tried to talk away the specificity of the universe. The reasonings of both groups were distinctly non-scientific.[35] Einstein's main achievement was to put cosmological discourse on truly scientific tracks. Here too misleading clichés abound. The heart of the cosmology which General Relativity made possible, is not whether the total mass of the universe is finite or not, or whether it is expanding or not, or whether its expansion would turn into a contraction or not, let alone whether the universe is 10 or 18 billion years old. The heart of that cosmology is the value, a most specific figure, which it is able to give about the space-time curvature valid for the entire universe. Most likely, that value is a small positive number, standing for the closed spherical net of permissible paths of motion, the new definition of space. But even if that curvature should turn out to be a small negative number, standing for a hyperbolic space, it should strike one with its specificity. Such a space can be illustrated by a saddle, with no edges, but with extremely well-defined slopes. The only possibility which is certainly excluded is Euclidean infinity whose curvature is 0, an age-old symbol of non-existence.[36]

Whatever has been learned about the cosmos since Einstein published in 1917 his cosmology provided further stunning details about the specificity of the universe in space as well as in time. In Prof. Weinberg's *First Three Minutes* there are some beautiful pages on that specific primordial soup which gave rise to the chemical elements on which all else, including our own specific existence, is based.[37] Specificity is the hallmark of all the avidly pursued cosmological research which pushed the study of the genesis of the universe beyond its baryon stage, described in the *First Three Minutes*. The earlier states investigated more recently are known as the lepton, hadron, quantum and matter-antimatter states. In those cases we see the same story: the story of one cosmic specificity leading to another, and in staggeringly exact and specific quantitative terms. In the matter-antimatter state, for instance, ordinary matter particles must outnumber antimatter particles in the specifically exact ratio of one part in ten billion to let subsequent physical interactions issue in processes characteristic of our actually observed specific universe.[38] At any stage, the slightest departure from the specificity as postulated would prevent the formation of galaxies and certainly the emergence of man. This is the consideration which made so many cosmologists for the past twenty years speak of the anthropic principle.[39] The principle stands for the nagging suspicion that the universe may indeed have been fashioned for the sake of man. Clearly, cosmologists are, in spite of themselves, in the grip of a meaning which stretches from the universe to man and from man to the universe and beyond.

There are of course brave, never-say-die warriors who try to undercut this most momentous outcome and perspective, which is replete with theology. Their efforts are either scientifically self-defeating, or scientifically revealing, or logically impossible. Into the first class belongs the now-defunct steady-state theory, whose proponents tried to save infinity for the universe along the time parameter only to pile infinite matter upon infinite matter since eternity. Into the second class belong the efforts which try to restore perfect homogeneity to the space-time manifold, or rather to the vacuum postulated by quantum field theory. In the context of such efforts one comes across baffling questions about the strangely specific ratios of physical forces and interactions and one finds revealing comments such as: "Some or all of these questions may not have answers. The world may be just the way it is."[40] The third class is made up by theories aimed at showing on *a priori* basis that the structure and extent of matter of the material world can only be what it is and nothing else. What these theories aim at is not a complete description and account of all known phenomena. This is in itself not impossible. The physical universe is thoroughly ordered and rational, if the findings of science have any meaning at all. The famed astronomer James Jeans made a notable muddle of philosophy, and even more of science, when he entertained the world with a once famous book, *The Mysterious Universe*.[41] Furthermore, it is not in itself impossible that one should by a lucky stroke of genius hit upon a mathematical formula which could deal not only with all known phenomena but would prove equally successful with all phenomena still to be discovered about the universe. Some theoreticians (the third class in question) dream about much more. They hope to construct a mathematical physics which would be equivalent to showing that the structure or specificity of the universe can only be what it is and nothing else. Such hopes, as I have kept insisting in published writings and in open oral debates for the past fifteen years, though apparently without creating any echo, should be viewed as logically impossible, as long as Gödel's incompleteness theorem is valid.[42] In other words, the specificity of the universe will remain the kind of specificity which keeps reminding any sensitive mind that it is not a necessary but a contingent feature, a specificity which does not have its *raison d'etre* in itself, but must depend on a choice external to the universe.

This is the very core of the message of modern cosmology about the universe. That most cosmologists are reluctant or simply unable to spell it out clearly, or take evasive action about it, does not matter. The message is there and is recognized by sensitive minds in private at least. Solovine, a friend of Einstein, shared his concern only with Einstein that Einstein's cosmology evoked the existence of a Creator. Nor did Einstein publish his reply which contained phrases, reassuring on a cursory look but full of strange uneasiness in between the lines: "I have not yet fallen in the hands of priests," Einstein wrote to his friend, and added: "Let the devil care what priests would do with my cosmology."[43]

What priests do with Einstein's cosmology, with his science of the universe, should not be of any concern here. What should be of concern here is what the universities are doing with the universe as revealed by twentieth-century scientific cosmology. For clearly, unless etymologies are completely misleading, the universe and the university cannot be foreign to one another. A university as an institution was born in the belief (a belief specific to the Middle Ages) that it is meaningful to search for universal knowledge, precisely because there is a universe, that is, a coherent totality of things and minds. Are universities still such institutions, or have they degenerated into places of entertainment where non-science students are initiated into twentieth-century cosmology through courses in which the mythology of extraterrestrial intelligence is presented with all the dazzling glamor of audio-visual techniques as the latest in respectable and reliable science?[44] Telling signs of intellectual degeneracy can also be gathered from the various concerns which aim at bridging the gap between the two cultures, the humanities and the sciences, and above all from the patently slick condition in which the humanities find themselves. Humanists blame as a rule the encroachment of the quantitative scientific method in all fields, even in fields where they have hardly anything applicable. Here humanists certainly have a valid point. Quantitative method, when applied exclusively in the field of values, leads to an erosion of meaning, an erosion which does not seem to worry many scientists secure in their chairs, laboratories, and shore-side bungalows. But others, especially the young who feel all too keenly uncertainties of all kinds, cannot be fooled. It was in all likelihood someone very familiar with the depersonalized atmosphere of modern universities who wrote the poignant lines:

> Lost in concrete canyons
> and captivated by our knowledge of science
> we tend to see God nowhere.[45]

Clearly, the young complained about lack of meaning. The great scouts of the canyons of science did not provide meaning, quantities in themselves never do. What about the humanists? Many of them turned into pseudo-humanists who blindly ape the scientists. They trust scientific data and computer printouts much more than their own minds and remain unaware of the third of the three kinds of lie: plain lie, big lie and statistics. Other humanists, the minority, still mindful of the mind, are largely demoralized. The result was put concisely in a comment on the Rockefeller report on "The Humanities in American Life": "Humanists have lost their franchise . . . Humanity goes on without the humanists."[46] If only humanity would go on, but obviously it does not. A mere look at the tensions, ready to rip apart the globe, although sprinkled all over by thousands of universities, should be enough of a proof. In fact, as a recent study showed, of all institutions it is the universities that most easily accommodate professional instigators of tensions.[47] It is all too obvious that humanists themselves have lost, by and large, confidence in meaning and for two reasons: One is that they have lost trust in human nature as something more than a machine. They simply caved in to scientism propagated by shallow scientists and scientifically uninformed philosophers. The second reason is that they have no close contact with that minority among leading scientists who are very sensitive to the limitations of the scientific method. But whether these remarks are right or wrong, the atmosphere of universities is hardly conducive to questions about meaning. Knowledge they certainly give, but the more they give the greater is the hunger for meaning.[48] To those ready to brand these remarks as the futile lamentations of a priest let me quote the Grand Master of Grand Orient in Paris. In connection with the sweeping changes effected in French universities by the Socialist government (13 of the 27 French universities have already received new rectors — a process which witnessed the replacement of Giscardian technocrats with social engineers) the Grand Master said: "We Freemasons do not accept the transformation of our universities into productivist establishments. The mission of universities is the teaching of the humanities and the sciences."[49]

The obvious failure of universities, the chief teaching institutions, to live up to the goal of the kind of teaching which is a search for meaning, that is, human understanding, is strongly suggestive of a situation which J. S. Mill described in prophetic words:

> When the philosophical minds of the world can no longer believe its religion or can only believe it with modifications amounting to an essential change of its character, a transitional period commences, of weak convictions, paralysed intellects, and growing laxity of principle, which cannot terminate until a renovation has been effected in the basis of their belief, leading to the evolution of some faith, whether religious or merely human, which they can really believe; and when things are in this state, all thinking or writing which does not tend to promote such a renovation, is of very little value beyond the moment.[50]

The new religion, or the new meaning, which Mill had in mind, was an outlook steeped in science. It may surprise you but I have no objection to this religion and for a very simple reason. The more genuine success is claimed by science, the more specific the universe will appear. Of course, any aspect of ordinary reality is very specific, specific to the point of being queer. The queer specificity of the real world immediately surrounding us, the everyday world, has a lasting freshness only to very sensitive onlookers and extraordinary minds. But the ordinary mind cannot help being startled when it finds the entire universe described by science in a few bafflingly specific terms. Even the ordinary mind would be awakened to the fact that such a specificity is hardly an exclusive possibility. Once this is realized, Creator, religion, and meaning emerge on the mental horizon and beckon for recognition. Had Chesterton lived to learn about modern cosmology, his always voluble enthusiasm would have overflown. For already in 1905 when he wrote his first major book, *Heretics*, he fully saw that the great disease and heresy of modern culture was its refusal to consider the general, that is, the meaning. Modern culture, as Chesterton put it, was lost in details and in a state of mind in which "everything matters - except everything,"[51] that is, the universe. Modern culture, precisely on account of its professional agnosticism if not plain paganism was in the straitjacket of a dogmatism which prescribed, to quote Chesterton again, that "Man may turn over and explore a million objects, but he must not find that strange object, the universe; for if he does, he will have a religion, and be lost."[52] If such was the case, and Mill, who spoke of cosmology as the stronghold of theists,[53] would certainly have agreed, then it followed, to paraphrase a remark of Chesterton, that once our students were given the universe, they would have religion.[54]

A better formulation of what should be the chief mission of a healthy university today to the sick world of today could hardly be put any better. The university must give the universe so that the world may have religion, or else the world will have a counterreligion, a much worse predicament than all the disasters which true religion may, in spite of itself, promote. Healthy universities would also find in Chesterton's *Heretics* a marvelous diagnosis of the inner logic which sets in today's universities at loggerheads two leading departments: the cosmologists and the biologists. The cosmologists, being in the grip of the specificity of the whole, will instinctively hand down a teaching very different from the one given by the biologists, who are all too often microbiologists. Concerned with the minutest details they can easily grow insensitive to the whole, that is, man and his search for meaning. "Before long," Chesterton prophesied in 1905, "the world will be cloven with a war between the telescopists and the microscopists."[55] The war, or conflict, is all too evident today. While cosmologists all too often are forced to face up to the question of meaning, posed by an unbelievably strange universe, biologists, especially their Darwinian kind, blissfully go on with their narrow strategy which leaves no room for questions about meaning. Typically, it is when they take a quick look at what their cosmologist colleagues are doing that it dawns suddenly on them that the strategy may be too superficial to secure ultimate victory for them. A most illuminating case of this occurs in the very first page of the very first chapter of Prof. Wilson's *On Human Nature*. The case is illuminating in more than one sense. While the illuminating force of cosmology can be sensed between the lines, each of those lines is a sad philosophical muddle:

If humankind evolved by Darwinian natural selection, genetic chance and environmental necessity, not God, made the species. Deity still can be sought in the origin of the ultimate units of matter, in quarks and electron shells (Hans Kung was right to ask atheists why there is something instead of nothing) but not in the origin of the species. However much we embellish that stark conclusion with metaphor and imagery, it remains the philosophical legacy of the last century of scientific research.[56]

A legacy which is the hybrid compound of chance and necessity is anything but philosphical. Neither Prof. Wilson, nor other Darwinists, and certainly not Prof. Monod or any of the members of the Copenhagen school of quantum mechanics, have ever given a philosophically satisfactory definition of chance.[57] The best definition of chance is still that it is a convenient cover for our ignorance. As to the crediting of Hans Küng with the specific question, why there is something rather than nothing, it is worthy of a scientist who knows theology only through the good services of the Book of the Month Club. Indeed the philosphical and theological poverty of Prof. Wilson's lines could not have been greater, a poverty typical of leading faculty of modern universities. For if indeed God, the ultimate in intelligibility and being, that is, meaning, can be sought in the origin of quarks, electron shells, 3° K radiation, over-all cosmic space-time curvature, in cosmology in short,[58] then the claim that the evolution of species is a meaningless chance process will have no foundation. Once there is a Creator, there can be no chance in the pseudo-ontological sense which Darwinists attribute to that word. They should above all remind themselves that if all is chance and necessity or both, then any scientific discoverer, and certainly any Nobel Prize winner, must carefully avoid crediting *himself* with any discovery, big and small.

Clear and cogent as this may be, acknowledgment of it will not come forth from most of the leading academics captivated by what they see through their microscopes. Even most of those who look through their telescopes will take refuge either in solipsism,[59] or in some variation of Bertrand Russell's claim that nothing forces man to look beyond the universe.[60] Nothing, of course, except the intellect insofar as the intellect is *non-*

mechanical, and thus it cannot be forced in a mechanical sense, not even in a sense which is touted to be logical but, like all equations of mechanics, is tautological because logic deals with strict identity relations. The most overrated and at the same time most explosive symbol of mathematical physics is that equation sign which states that nothing happens unless something is already happening. In the absence, or rather precisely because of the absence of mechanical necessity in the process of demonstration, the confrontation of believers and non-believers will go on. Let us hope that, in the best interest of those on both sides, it will go on in that liberal spirit which is not blind to the difference between liberty and licentiousness.

In all likelihood only a minority of universities, committed by their statutes and strengthened by their loyalty to those statutes or hallowed mottos, will teach not only information but also meaning, that is, true integral humanness. I hope and pray that this University will never be ashamed of a reference in its statutes to Jesus Christ as a unique revelation of God. I am saying this not only as a theologian but also as a historian of science. Only the professedly rationalist and materialist historians of science keep ignoring that belief in creation out of nothing played a pivotal role in the formulation, in the 14th century, of some crucial notions anticipating and preparing Newtonian physics. It is still to gain broad awareness that without the dogma of Incarnation, according to which only the Son is begotten and therefore the world cannot be a begetting or an eternal, necessary part of God, the dogma of creation out of nothing would have lost much of its incisiveness.[61] But history of science or not, the incomparable fact of Christ demands the careful study on the part of all those who in this age of science put the highest premium on unconditional respect for facts. Such a respect is easier to say than to implement. I wonder whether T. H. Huxley ever did with respect to Christ what he urged with respect to any fact of Nature: sit down before fact like a child and follow its voice no matter where it may lead.[62]

Teachers at universities where integral humanness is the supreme standard will have plenty of opportunities to take heart from the slips of tongue all too frequent in universities where hallowed mottos (*Novum Testamentum-Vetus Tes-*

tamentum, In numine Dei viget, etc. . . .) have degenerated into mere slips of tongue. Such a slip of tongue is a remark of Prof. Wilson that religion cannot be eliminated because like everything else, it too is a matter of genes in whose subservience we allegedly all are.[63] Such a slip of tongue is that popular Harvard course, which has been dubbed "Guilt 33" by the undergraduates.[64] Its two teachers organized it under the impact of having discovered that children, never exposed to religion, all too often develop a sense of guilt in a genuinely moral sense. Such slips of tongue are indicative of that sheepish manner in which a dehumanized science reinstates man, the religious animal, and bows to the truth of *anima naturaliter Christiana.* Thus, when teachers in universities committed to meaning feel downcast by their minority status, let them take heart from the fact that they will be the last consistent defenders not only of the humanities but also of true science. Or as Chesterton put it at the end of his *Heretics:*

> We shall be left defending not only the incredible virtues and sanities of human life, but something more incredible still, this huge impossible universe which stares us in the face. We shall fight for visible prodigies as if they were invisible. We shall look on the impossible grass and skies with a strange courage. We shall be of those who have seen and yet have believed.[65]

NOTES

1. John H. Newman, *The Idea of a University Defined and Illustrated* (8th ed.; London: Longmans Green and Co., 1888), p. 145.
2. The remark, probably made in December 1871 at a meeting in New York of Williams alumni, provided the title for R. Frederick's book, *Mark Hopkins and the Log: Williams College, 1836-1872* (New Haven: Yale University Press, 1956).
3. Letter of April 11, 1892, to Prof. E. Ray Lankester, in *The Life and Letters of Thomas Henry Huxley,* by L. Huxley (New York: D. Appleton, 1901), vol. II, p. 328. The "factory of

knowledge" stood in contrast to the "storehouse of knowledge," or the medieval university.

4. A favorite remark of Sir George Pickering, Regius Professor of Medicine in Oxford University.

5. For a long list of no less shocking topics of theses that earned Ph.D., see A. Flexner, *Universities: American, English, German* (1930; reprinted with a new introduction by C. Kerr; New York: Oxford University Press, 1968), pp. 153-54.

6. Unidentified author, quoted in *A New Dictionary of Quotations on Historical Principles from Ancient and Modern Sources*, selected and edited by H. L. Mencken (New York: Alfred A. Knopf, 1946), p. 1238.

7. Ibid.

8. *The Idea of a University*, p. 145.

9. Thomas Carlyle in his fifth lecture, "The Hero as Man of Letters. Johnson, Rousseau, Burns," delivered on May 19, 1840, in the series, *On Heroes, Hero-Worship and the Heroic in History*.

10. Newman would find even more revolting the custom of taking these words of President Wilson out of context. In his speech given before the Y.M.C.A. of Pittsburgh on October 24, 1914, Wilson started with a reference to his experience as president of Princeton University that students far from being "arch radicals" were markedly conservative, resisting any change relating to instruction and campus life. Worse, they were most unwilling to admit their strong attachment to their fathers' outlook, limited in most cases to their business or profession. Hence the need, stressed by Wilson, to expose young men to the far and wide world of ideas and make them "as unlike their fathers as possible." The main thrust of Wilson's speech is hardly ever quoted. Indeed, presidents of Christian colleges and universities would for the most part be very unwilling to insist nowadays on an atmosphere in their campuses which Wilson believed to permeate Y.M.C.A. clubs. After their initial hostility to Y.M.C.A., most churches realized, Wilson stated, that "it was a common instrument for sending the light of Christianity out into the world in its most practical form, drawing young men who were strangers into places

where they could have companionship that stimulated them and suggestions that kept them straight and occupations that amused them without vicious practices; and then, by surrounding themselves with an atmosphere of *purity and of simplicity of life*, catch something of a glimpse of the great ideal which *Christ lifted* when he was elevated *upon the Cross.*" Quotations are from the text of Wilson's speech, printed by the U.S. Government Printing Office, in a ten-page-long pamphlet, No. 67334-14. See especially, pp. 3 and 4-5 (Italics added).

11. A remark in Henry Fielding's comedy, *The Temple Beau* (1730); see *The Works of Henry Fielding* (new ed.; London: J. Johnson, 1806), vol. I, p. 192. Fielding, much better remembered for his *Tom Jones*, would find many more tragic than hilarious incidents in the mores prevailing in most modern campuses.

12. In the sense, of course, that natural theology provided a rational justification of the possibility of revealed truth. Newman, who delivered in 1852 the nine lectures forming *The Idea of a University*, stressed the intellectual indispensability of natural theology in the face of fideism which he knew all too well from his Protestant years and which also made heavy inroads into Catholic theology during the decades of Romanticism. Newman's insistence on natural theology was a prophetic anticipation of the Thomistic revival stressed by Leo XIII and his successors. While the demise of natural theology, during the last two decades, in most Catholic colleges and universities would have dismayed him, he would see it as a logical consequence of the betrayal there of the philosophical ideas of Thomas Aquinas.

13. S. Weinberg, *The First Three Minutes: A Modern View of the Origin of the Universe* (London: Andre Deutsch, 1977), p. 154.

14. References are to the Bantam Book edition (New York, 1979). See pp. 3 and 217.

15. Ibid., p. [ii]

16. Ibid., p. xi.

17. See Max F. Schulz, *The Poetic Voices of Coleridge: A Study of His Desire for Spontaneity and Passion for Order* (Detroit:

Wayne State University Press, 1963). Schulz marshalled strong evidence against the view that at least some books of Coleridge were the products of "manual somnambulism" (p . 7).

18. A. N. Whitehead, *The Function of Reason* (Princeton: Princeton University Press, 1929), p. 12.

19. A. Einstein, "Physics and Reality" (1936) in *Out of My Later Years* (New York: Philosophical Library, 1950), p. 59.

20. For details, see ch. 12, in my *The Road of Science and the Ways to God*, The Gifford Lectures, 1974-75 and 1975-76 (Chicago: University of Chicago Press, 1978).

21. Reported by E. Gilson in his *D'Aristote a Darwin et retour: Essai sur quelques constantes de la biophilosophie* (Paris: Vrin, 1973), p. 49.

22. A truth, which was given new popularity in our time by Sir Karl Popper, although his philosophy can hardly accommodate a science of cosmology properly so-called.

23. For details, see my *The Road of Science*, pp. 121-22.

24. It was Kant's exposure to Rousseau's *Julie* and *Emile* in 1762 that crystallized his groping for that autonomy. For details, see my book *Angels, Apes and Men* (La Salle, Ill.: Sherwood Sugden, 1982); ch. 1.

25. A vast documentary evidence on behalf of this claim is given in the introduction and notes to my translation of Kant's cosmogony, *A Universal Natural History and Theory of the Heavens* (Edinburgh: Scottish Academic Press, 1981).

26. See *Angels, Apes and Men* (ch. 3) and my earlier publications, *The Paradox of Olbers' Paradox* (New York: Herder and Herder, 1969), pp. 158-60 and "Das Gravitations-Paradoxon des unendlichen Universums," *Sudhoffs Archiv* 63 (1979), pp. 105-22.

27. Not even K. Schwarzschild's two discussions; in 1901 and 1908, in terms of four-dimensional geometry, of the relation of the total mass, supposedly confined to the Milky Way, and to the empty space surrounding it. See my *Milky Way: An Elusive Road for Science* (New York: Science History Publications, 1972), p. 276.

28. For details, see E. Gilson, "Theology and the Unity of Knowledge," in L. Leary (ed.), *The Unity of Knowledge*

(Garden City, N.Y.: Doubleday, 1955), pp. 40-42.

29. For details, see the introduction to my translation of Bruno's *The Ash Wednesday Supper: La cena de le ceneri* (The Hague: Mouton, 1975).

30. For details, see *Universal Natural History and Theory of the Heavens*, pp. 280-81.

31. That the law of the instability of the homogeneous, the primary principle in Spencer's cosmogony, never appeared to him intrinsically contradictory, may have its explanation in his candid admission, "I am never puzzled." See *Autobiography* (New York: D. Appleton, 1904), vol. I, p. 462.

32. This is certainly true of the Laplacian version of that nebula and of the popular or cliché version of Kant's dicta on the subject. Actually, Kant in his cosmogonical work carefully specified the initial condition, which in his belief gave rise to the actual shape of the universe.

33. As can readily be gathered from his notebooks composed in 1837-38. For details see *Angels, Apes and Men*, Ch. 2.

34. Part of that story is the Marxist espousal of the doctrine of eternal recurrence. See my *From Eternal Cycles to an Oscillating Universe* (Edinburgh: Scottish Academic Press, 1974), pp. 312-18.

35. See my *The Paradox of Olbers' Paradox* ch. 9 and *The Milky Way*, ch. 8.

36. On some apt comments on the significance of zero, see my article, "The Chaos of Scientific Cosmology," in *The Nature of the Physical Universe: 1976 Nobel Conference*, organized by Gustavus Adolphus College, edited by D. Huff and O. Prewett (New York: John Wiley: 1979), p. 92.

37. Especially, pp. 102-08. For somewhat different figures, see B. Lovell, *In the Centre of Immensities* (London: Hutchinson, 1979), pp. 120-26.

38. Such an inference can be made on the basis of the finding which earned to V. Fitch and J. Cronin the Nobel Prize, that for two out of every thousand artificially induced decays of neutral K_2 mesons, symmetry laws do not hold.

39. For an early statement, see B. Carter, "Large Number Coincidences and the Anthropic Principle is Cosmology," in M.S. Longair (ed), *Confrontation of Cosmological Theories with Observational Data* (Dordrecht: D. Reidel, 1974), pp. 291-98.

40. M. B. Wise, H. Georgi, and S. L. Glashow, "SU(5) and the Indivisible Axion," *Physical Review Letters* 47 (August 10, 1981), p. 402.

41. The philosophical shallowness of that book was held up to a well-deserved criticism by L. S. Stebbing, *Philosophy and the Physicists* (London: Methuen, 1958).

42. For the first time in my *The Relevance of Physics* (Chicago: University of Chicago Press, 1966), pp. 127-30.

43. See Letters of Jan. 1, 1951 and March 30, 1952 in *Lettres á Maurice Solovine* (Paris: Gauthiers-Villars, 1956), pp. 102 and 115.

44. Students are hardly ever made aware of the true thrust of Carl Sagan's studied reliance on the use of triple and at times quadruple negatives.

45. Quoted in M. Link, *Take off Your Shoes* (New York: Paulist Press, 1974), p. 40.

46. Words of B. Murchland, quoted in *Newsweek* (October 13, 1980), p. 113. The report itself, *The Humanities in American Life* (Berkeley: University of California Press, 1980), is noteworthy for its sedulous avoidance of any philosophical question that may arise in connection with man and mankind.

47. I have in mind studies prepared recently at the University of Aberdeen by Professor P. Wilkinson. See especially his "Proposals for Governments and International Responses to Terrorism," in P. Wilkinson (ed.), *British Perspectives on Terrorism* (London: George Allen & Unwin, 1981).

48. The phenomenon is not at all new. What is new is the inability of an ever larger number of students to articulate, however simply, their intensely felt need for meaning. Quite a difference with respect to the 1950's when seventy-eight percent of almost 8,000 students selected from 48 colleges and universities stated in a survey conducted by social scientists that their main goal in education was the finding of meaning and purpose to life. See V. E. Frankl, *Man's Search for Meaning: An Introduction to Logotherapy* (New York: Simon and Schuster, 1963), p. 55.

49. *Le Monde* (Aug. 13, 1982), p. 5, from an interview with R. Leroy, grand-master.

50. J. S. Mill, *Autobiography*, with an introduction by C. V.

Shields (Indianapolis: Bobbs-Merrill, 1957), p. 153.

51. G. K. Chesterton, *Heretics* (London: John Lane, 1905), p. 13.

52. Ibid.

53. Mill, *Autobiography*, p. 145. That Mill speaks actually of mathematical and physical sciences, should pose no problem. Nor should his lumping of theists with idealists; Mill merely confused metaphysics with idealism.

54. *Heretics*, p. 13.

55. Ibid., p. 51.

56. *On Human Nature*, p. 200.

57. As I argued in my "Chance or Reality: Interaction in Nature and Measurements in Physics," PHILOSOPHIA (Athens) 10-11 (1980-81), pp. 85-102.

58. As acknowledged by Prof. Wilson, *On Human Nature*, pp. 1 and 200.

59. The number of such astronomers and cosmologists is much larger than suspected.

60. A claim memorably stressed in his debate with Fr. Copleston on the existence of God.

61. A discussion and documentation of this point can be found in my *Cosmos and Creator* (Edinburgh: Scottish Academic Press, 1981), pp. 65-79.

62. "Sit down before fact as a little child, be prepared to give up every preconceived notion, follow humbly wherever and to whatever abysses nature leads, or you shall learn nothing." *Life and Letters of Thomas Henry Huxley*, vol. I, p. 219. These words are part of a letter (Sept. 23, 1860), in which Huxley declined the suggestion that following the death of his seven-year-old son, he should consider the message of Christ about immortality. One wonders whether the thought had crossed Huxley's mind that what he urged with respect to facts, Christ most emphatically urged with respect to Himself when He singled out children as the ones possessed of the proper attitude toward His Kingdom. At any rate, it was typical of Huxley, the natural scientist, that for him the realm of facts did not really include the very real facts of human history.

63. *On Human Nature*, p. 42.

64. The official entry for the course is "Literature and Arts

A-20" and has the title, "The Literature of Christian Reflection," taught by Dr. Robert Coles and Prof. Robert Kiely. The course seems to offer much more to young men and women looking for meaning, than, for instance, the course described in the catalogue of Harvard Divinity School as "Applied Theology 142. Sociology of Religion and Teaching. This is a macro/micro humanistic approach to the sociology of religion and teaching containing four components: (1) Examination of historical paradigms; (2) Field studies of radical sociological change in religious states; (3) Analysis of social-cultural continuities and discontinuities, derived and underived religious posturing, dimensions of tension, crisis confluence and synthesis in cross-cultural states; (4) A correlation of sociology and teaching enabling the student to distill transcendent processes as well as to develop a more cogent language of religion in the context of educational goals." To this the best reaction still is the *New Yorker's* comment: "Those who pass, go straight to Heaven" (Feb. 26, 1979, p. 103, col. 1).

65. *Heretics*, p. 305.

Chapter 5

Early Christianity and Society: A Contemporary Academic Interest

ABRAHAM J. MALHERBE

There are periods in the history of academic disciplines when fundamental reassessments are made of the presuppositions and shapes of the disciplines, and when new directions are charted. The study of early Christianity has during the last decade undergone such introspection and has developed new interests and methods of investigation which have spawned new journals, new research seminars and teams in learned societies, and newly conceived graduate programs. These developments have taken place primarily in this country, and that for two major reasons: The vitality in scholarship which has moved here from Europe, and the growth in numbers and size of departments of religious studies in publicly supported colleges and universities. Scholars in such departments, but not only they, have begun to address questions raised by colleagues in the social sciences and literary criticism, for example, rather than by theologians.

One of the major current interests is in the social history of early Christianity. In the late nineteenth and early twentieth centuries students of Christian origins did devote considerable attention to the social dimension of early Christianity and did so mainly out of Marxist and romantic interests. It is probably correct to say that the concern for the most part was with the social description of the emerging church rather than with social theory, although the developing social sciences were pressed into service from time to time. The situation today is more diverse. There are those who are content with social description, but a whole new generation of younger scholars are attempting to convince the guild of the importance of contemporary social theory.

Both approaches, that of social description and of social theory, have been hampered because their practitioners have lacked the competencies demanded by the agendas they set for themselves. Those interested in social theory have generally not been trained in it and, according to critics in a position to know, have frequently ended up mining the social sciences in an eclectic, if not downright amateurish manner. Too few have even faced the question whether the ancient texts, which are the material with which they have to work, lend themselves to the kinds of analysis and construction of modern sociology, which are based on living, observable religious communities.

My own interest is in social history rather than in the application of contemporary social theory to early Christianity, and I shall confine my remarks to this part of the endeavor. The social historian may have better prospects, but is at present not much better off. He too is dependent on the texts and needs to develop competencies that have been neglected. Students of early Christianity have for so long read the texts with theological or ecclesiastical interests that they do not even recognize the social dimensions of their material. The identification of sociological data, not to speak of their interpretation, requires competencies which should not be viewed as new to the student of Christian origins, but which have in fact become sorely neglected.

It would seem self-evident that the student of early Christianity would be well-trained in the languages, literature and culture of Greek and Roman antiquity, but today that is no longer the case, and liberal arts colleges are partly to be blamed. Classics departments, where they have been allowed to exist, have not been faithful to their heritage. For understandable reasons, their offerings of classical civilization courses, which require no knowledge of Greek or Latin, are designed for the student body at large, who are thus enticed to satisfy distributive requirements in the humanities by taking broadly conceived courses which teem with generalizations. At the other extreme, it has become possible to specialize so early in one's college career, and so narrowly, that neither a sound foundation nor sufficient perspective is developed to support serious advanced work. Colleges supported by certain Roman Catholic orders and conservative Protestants have in general done a better job of teaching the languages, although this generalization holds less true these days, but they have not succeeded in producing classicists with that combination of imagination and discipline that one expects from first rate liberal arts programs.

It is clear that no great advances on a broad front will be made in writing the social history of early Christianity until the basic disciplines have brought their houses in order and have again been given pride of place in the preparation of future scholars. In the meantime, progress will be made slowly as remedial work is undertaken with graduate students and as more mature scholars themselves retool. I am not, of course, suggesting that very little of value is being done, or that the results of recent work have been few. By way of illustrating what has been done, I still draw attention to new perceptions that have emerged from recent investigation of the social level of early Christians and the nature of their communities, and shall draw the implications of this for Christian attitudes toward society.

Until recently, the view was commonly held that the earliest Christians came from the lowest social classes. In this, Marxist and romantic agreed. Karl Kautsky, the Marxist historian of socialism, thought of early Christians as proletarian, un-educated, oppressed and far removed from the masses of the people. Their doctrine and history, he maintained, were con-fined to esoteric oral traditions which could not be tested by outsiders. Originally prompted by economic and social distress, as Christianity gradually attracted people from the Roman administrative classes, it developed its own ruling class in the hierarchy. Adolph Deissmann, the German Protestant romantic, did not reject Kautsky's description of the Christians, but attributed to Kautsky's "sated Berlin rationalism" the latter's refusal to credit Jesus with the conception of Christianity. For

Deissmann, Christianity was "a movement among the weary and heavy-laden, men without power and position, 'babes' as Jesus himself calls them, the poor, the base, the foolish, as St. Paul with a prophet's sympathy describes them." Deissmann's reference is to I Corinthians 1:26, "For consider your call brethren; not many of you were wise according to worldly standards, not many were powerful, not many were of noble birth." Even the level of Greek used by early Christians was for Deissmann an index of their lowly status.

Recent investigations have come to see matters quite differently. While admitting that Paul indicates that not many of his converts were intellectuals, politicians or persons of noble birth, they insist that his words suggest that at least some persons of such status were to be found in his churches. And, what is more significant, the evidence is thought to suggest that they were a dominating minority. Attention has consequently been drawn to the different classes of persons represented in the churches, and to individuals within the churches. Not content with generalizations about Christianity as a whole, scholars have investigated particular Christian communities with special interest in the status and role of individuals within them. I offer some of the results of these investigations, confining myself to Paul, about whom and about whose churches we know most.

Paul is known to have received a typical Jewish upbringing in Jerusalem, and this fact has sometimes led to dislocating him from the Greek society in which he established his churches. However, the Paul we know as the founder of churches had already been engaged in missionary work for roughly two decades by the time he wrote the letters we now have. These letters are our oldest primary sources for primitive Christianity. They reveal a person who does not write the so-called common Greek, but what has been named professional prose, a type of Greek used when a writer's primary concern was to communicate rather than to produce a document of literary distinction. In sections of his major letters Paul also adopts the style of the diatribe, which had been developed in the philosophical school, and puts it to his own use in argumentation. As to their form and character, the letters themselves are the products of a creative genius who transcended the epistolary clichés of his day to produce a new literary genre. They reflect the kind of activity that belongs to the give and take of discussion rather than the pulpit or the street corner.

Closer investigation of his missionary method has been thought to reveal that he founded groups who would be viewed by his contemporaries as under the patronage of relatively well-off individuals. Like Paul himself, these persons are thought to have enjoyed social status in society. They included not only such itinerant business persons as Lydia the dealer in purple and Aquila and Priscilla, the traders in tents, but Erastus the city treasurer of Corinth. Such persons provided the setting for Paul's teaching, space for the meetings of the churches he founded, and they extended hospitality to traveling members of the faith. Although the churches began among people of this economic and social class, they soon became highly stratified, with the majority of their members coming from the less favoured classes. Nevertheless, the letters of Paul, addressed to these churches, portray groups in which the more socially prominent individuals had an importance beyond their numbers.

Undoubtedly these churches met for worship, but it is striking how little detail Paul's letters supply about worship practices. In contrast, the letters address theological and ethical issues with unfailing regularity and extended exposition or debate. Since these letters were written to be read publicly in the assemblies, it is not surprising that the churches have recently been described as scholastic communities. With few exceptions, the worship of the churches was regarded as a constant which could be assumed and which required little comment or correction. It could be assumed to provide a common basis for discussing other aspects of the Christian life which had constantly to be worked out, elaborated or refined. In addition to the theological discussions which were occasioned by reflection on the initial missionary teaching or by contrary views espoused by competing wandering preachers, one reads over and over again of tensions within the heterogeneous communities. Personal relationships between persons of different social status and financial means, intellectual ability, religious conviction and ethical norms, were constantly strained, and Paul had to address them. The intracommunal issues witness to communities in constant ferment, far different from the placid fellowships to which the harried of society fled, as an earlier, more romantic generation thought. The churches were not made up of stained glass saints, but of people who brought their problems and ambitions into the fellowships which they joined.

By becoming a Christian one did not escape the world, for the little fellowships were not conventicles isolated from society. To begin with, for the first hundred years of its history Christianity was overwhelmingly urban. Only gradually did it spread to the countryside, to the *pagani*, the pagans or rural folk, who were the last in a region to be converted. The earliest churches were established, for the most part, in large cities on the major trade routes of the Roman Empire. These cities were commercial and cultural centers, and attracted people of all classes, religions and cultures. Furthermore, they were open to an almost incredible variety of people from Egypt and the East who were wending their way to Rome. The archaeological and literary evidence shows us that in such cities the populace tended to be open to new influences and that they were inquisitive about new groups. Native residents in such cities may quite generally have had the attitude of the old codger in northern Vermont who still referred to people who had moved in from Massachusetts ten years earlier as "permanent summer people," but they watched the newcomers closely, especially if the exotic groups converted some local folk, and particularly if the converts came from the ranks of the prominent, as they often did. Christianity, as such a religion, could not escape attention any more than could Jews or the devotees of Isis.

It used to be fashionable to describe the loneliness of travelers in the ancient world, and to sketch a picture of strangers flocking to clubs and other sorts of fraternities to escape the impersonal existence in the large cities. Such a picture is hardly supported by the evidence. If anything, life in the typical city was too public, with people crowding in on you from every side. When you were likely to live in an apartment building, buy your hot water from the espresso stand downstairs, use the public sanitation facilities across the street and the public baths around the corner, were enlisted by the local block association to help settle disputes among neighbors or were dragged before such community tribunals by persons whom you offended, when you were subject to a constant stream of peddlers and candidates for office, and had to settle with the tax man with dismaying regularity, you were hardly lonely or neglected.

The conditions of ancient urban society sound quite familiar to us. Overcrowding was common, as was the attending organization of interest groups to secure their benefits or perceived rights. People organized themselves along national, professional and religious lines as well as others in order to exercise political influence as much as they did for other reasons. The question of allegiance, whether it was to be granted to the state or the larger common good rather than to the smaller unit of which one was a part, had constantly to be faced. The cities' economies were in perpetual difficulty. Natural disasters such as plagues and famines played their part in unsettling things, as did the sometimes ruthless competition between cities. Added to this were the large numbers of transients, many of them non-Greeks and non-Romans, who were taxing the resources of the cities and straining the social fabric. That public assistance was extended to them would not endear them to the native residents who might already be complaining that their own needs were not being met. Social institutions, especially marriage and the family, were breaking down despite repeated legislation which attempted vainly to protect them. Public as well as sexual morality were of concern not only to legislators, but also to the popular philosophers who sought the moral reformation of individuals and society.

This is the kind of setting in which the churches came into existence, and these conditions are reflected in Paul's letters to his churches. The churches' influential members were involved in commerce and local government. Furthermore, they were hardly likely to have been provincial in outlook, for they appear to have traveled as often as their contemporaries did. For example, half of the members of the Corinthian church whose names we know, we meet in the New Testament while they are away from home. Nor did people always convert as entire families; a major problem early Christians faced was that spouses often remained pagans. Some of the churches' members were also fairly well off while others lacked basic necessities and had become accustomed to being financially dependent.

From all sides, therefore, the life of the pagan city pressed in on the church, and it was faced with two temptations, either simply to be content with reflecting society's conditions and standards, or to withdraw completely. It chose neither option.

Christian literature from the first hundred years of the church's existence is entirely esoteric, that is, it is directed to the church rather than the larger society. These writings aim at the development of Christian individuals and communities by urging them to give practical expression to the doctrines they had accepted. Christian values, grounded religiously and theologically, were to govern Christian personal, institutional and social morality. Members of these small voluntary societies were expected to adhere to the norms under which they had placed themselves. An awareness of the distinction between Christians and the larger society is reflected in the designation of the latter as "outsiders". The border was important for the self-preservation of the group and its members, and was secured by church discipline. Social standards or behavior in conflict with those of the Christian community were not allowed to permeate the border. When they did, the guilty party was removed from the group which was striving to develop and maintain its peculiar identity.

One could expect that such an attitude would result in Christian smugness about their own superiority and that it could have led to complete withdrawal from society. Other contemporary groups did precisely that. Paul, however, did not allow his churches to act in this manner. Withdrawal was not a possibility. Christians, he says, may associate with "outsiders," however riddled they might be with vice, otherwise Christians "would need to go out of the world" (I Corinthians 5:9, 10), an option that is obviously beyond consideration. But when Paul draws the line between Christians and "outsiders" it is not to make the Christians proud; on the contrary, it is to shame them because they are not bringing to realization the capacity for the sanctified life which is theirs. Christians are called to self-judgment; God will judge the "outsiders" (I Corinthians 5:1, 12f). Sketched in this way, the impression may erroneously be gained that Paul's ethics was primarily personal, and that in his view Christian norms were radically different from those of the larger society. The impression is strengthened by the fact that Paul prohibits the church from taking intramural squabbles before pagan tribunals (I Corinthians 6). To illustrate Paul's view and the contribution that recent sociological studies can make to understanding him, I shall now confine myself to one example.

As a means of financial self-support, Paul on occasion engaged in manual labor as a tent-maker, a practice he draws attention to a number of times. He also urges his converts to work with their hands. Manual labor is an important topic in his letters to the Thessalonians, which are the basis for most of the following comments. As to his own practice, the traditional interpretation has been that Paul's trade could be explained by his rabbinic training, which encouraged teachers to acquire an appropriate trade, and that Paul worked at it in order not to burden his converts (as he indeed says he did, cf. II Corinthians 12:9; I Thessalonians 2:9). The Jewishness of the practice is then seen to set Paul over against the Greeks, who are thought to have despised manual labor. It is this aversion to work, it has been thought, exacerbated by an expectation of the imminent return of Christ and thus the end of the world order, that was the reason for the Thessalonians' idleness and Paul's consequent command that they work and be dependent on nobody. This interpretation is partly erroneous and completely inadequate in its grasp of the sophistication with which Paul argues or the social implications of his practice and argument. It is not simply a case of Jewish versus Greek ethos or of theological mis-understanding or pragmatic behavior.

Appeal to rabbinic discussion of the teacher's manual labor to illuminate Paul's practice is anachronistic, for the relevant information on the rabbinic discussions comes from a period much later than Paul and, furthermore, the rabbi working to support himself remained an elusive ideal. In Paul's day, on the other hand, the philosophical teacher's means of support was fervently debated by the Greeks and Romans. Elsewhere in I Thessalonians 2:1-8 Paul describes his work in terms used by those philosophers to describe the ideal philosopher, and his comments on his own work should be seen in that light as well as what he says elsewhere about his apostleship. The ideal philosopher, in this view, would work with his hands so that his disciples would see in him an example of the philosophically informed practical life. Furthermore, since manual labor was not held in high esteem, his practice would demonstrate the philosopher's disregard for convention when popular values were opposed to his task. The practice, therefore, drove to the heart of the philosopher's understanding of his task. So does Paul's practice.

In the contexts in his letters in which he makes much of his working with his hands, Paul does not idealize it. On the contrary, he couples manual labor with self-denial of rights (I Corinthians 9:15-18), offers it as an example of abasement (II Corinthians 11:7), and alludes to it as servile (I Corinthians 9:19). This is the attitude toward work of the classes which looked down upon it, the persons of some social status with whom Paul is increasingly being associated. The way in which Paul relates his practice to his understanding of his own mission demonstrates his knowledge of several traditions and his originality in argumentation. In I Corinthians 9:15-23, after intoning his right to financial support, he makes much of his willingness to forego it, and his argument is a sophisticated blend of Old Testament imagery, Stoic argument and Pauline paradox. Like the Old Testament prophet, he claims to have been divinely commissioned to his task so that he could not escape from it. But, using the language of Stoic discussions of determinism and free will, he says that while he did not have the freedom to reject his calling, he was free to decide how to give himself to the task. That freedom of decision was exhibited in not insisting on the rights which came with the inexorable call, but precisely in foregoing them. The logical move, as is the language, is quite Stoic, but not so is the characteristic Pauline paradox that then follows: Although he is free from all men, by undertaking to support himself by servile labor he enslaves himself in order to benefit all. The Paul who argues here is a person who looks at something as mundane as manual labor in religious, philosophical and theological terms. By not receiving financial support he is not simply bowing to practical considerations; his refusal of it is as much part of his self-understanding as it is that of the philosophers. And an awareness of the place of the philosophers in society and their attitudes to it enables us better to appreciate Paul's line of argument.

As Paul relates work to his own, apostolic, responsibility, he also relates it to the Thessalonians' responsibility. His practice confronts them with twin examples of considerateness and responsibility. Macedonia, the Roman province in which Thessalonica was a major city, experienced severe economic hardship during the mid-first century. The churches were poor, and it is not unexpected that financial matters take up as much space as they do in Paul's letters associated with Macedonia. Nor is it surprising that in the first two letters which we have from his pen, I and II Thessalonians, Paul should treat the matter at such length. These letters were written months after the church had been established, and there is a freshness about them as they take up issues confronting a newly founded church in a Greek city.

Paul is concerned with manual labor as it affects relationships within the church as well as between the church and the larger society, the "outsiders." That the means of support discussed in these letters is manual labor does not mean that the membership was constituted wholly of the lowest classes. II Thessalonians 3 indicates that the idlers, whose alternative was to work with their hands, sponged off others, presumably well-off persons, some of whom at least were members of the church. What is clear is that Paul in the first place addresses those who voluntarily have become dependent on others.

For those within the church, Paul recalls his own example of not burdening them. Just as he had not insisted on the apostolic prerogative of being harsh and demanding, but had been gentle as a nurse, and had given himself to them as a father to his children, so he had refused to burden them with financial demands (I Thessalonians 2:6-12). Paul mentions all this in a section of the letter where he reminds them of his unselfishness and considerateness. On the other hand, elsewhere he avers that his financial independence in his first contact with them was designed to be an example for them to follow: They were to be productive and not burdensome to each other (II Thessalonians 2:9-12). We do not know why the Thessalonian Christians were given to idleness. It is not explicitly related to their eschatological expectations, and in any case, Paul had offered them his own example to follow before they could have developed the views sometimes assumed to have been responsible for their idleness. It is quite possible, and I think likely, that they brought into the Christian community attitudes common in society, that well-off patrons and the state would provide for their needs. It is striking that when Paul seeks to correct such an attitude, he does not do so with an argument fraught with theological complexities as his discussion of his own apostleship is. Rather, he does so with an apodictic "If anyone will not work, let him not eat!" (II Thessalonians 3:10), which has the ring of marketplace bias.

In sum, with respect to relations within the church, labor is discussed in terms of deference to others, but much more so in terms of social responsibility. This should in no way be taken to suggest that Paul's insistence on working excludes the responsibility of helping those in genuine need. His commands are directed to those who have the realistic option of working. Lest their interpretation of his words lead to self-justification not to help those in need, he concludes his discussion of the subject with the command, "Brethren, do not be weary in well-doing" (II Thessalonians 3:13). The Book of Acts (20:34, 35) represents Paul as saying, "You yourselves know that these hands ministered to my necessities, and to those who were with me. In all things I have shown you that by so toiling one must help the weak, remembering the words of the Lord Jesus, how he said, 'It is more blessed to give than to receive'." It is because this compassion could be assumed that the problem arose in the first place, and that Paul has to stress individual responsibility.

The treatment of the relationship between the church and society as it touches on economic independence is more interesting (I Thessalonians 4:9-12). In his directions to the church on the matter, Paul again shows that he knows philosophical discussions about the attitudes of small communities toward society, in particular, the attitudes of Epicurean philosophers. He draws on these discussions as he moves from intramural concerns to the relationship between the church and society. He begins by saying that Christians are to love one another because they are taught by God to do so. The Greek word used to describe this divine instruction is of striking construction and in Greek literature appears here for the first time. It is a

Pauline coinage and stresses the divine will as the basis for ethics. In Thessalonian society such a theological grounding for ethics would be notable. Paul had made the connection between religion and ethics repeatedly in the preceding verses, so that this statement is part of a larger emphasis. But then, from speaking of divinely taught love in the Christian community, he goes on to tell them "to make it your ambition to live quietly, to mind your own affairs, and to work with your hands, as we charged you, so that you may command the respect of outsiders, and be dependent on nobody." Thus, when Paul gives concrete directions for social behavior, he abandons theological warrants and becomes rather prosaic — or so it seems.

In fact, however, Paul's language demonstrates his familiarity with philosophers' attitudes toward society, and he deliberately rejects one such attitude as not viable for the little church. The Epicureans, who also formed small communities, regarded friendship (the Pauline "brotherly love") among their members as the basis for their communal life. As friends they banded together, supporting each other financially, minded their own affairs, and withdrew from society. Taking no part in public affairs, they eschewed political ambition and had no concern for the approval of outsiders. It is not surprising that they were severely criticized in antiquity, partly for their withdrawal from and disregard for society.

From the standpoint of an outsider, Christianity and Epicureanism appeared similar in many respects: They were considered atheistic, because they rejected the popular religion, misanthropic, socially irresponsible, and immoral. It is only to be expected that pagan critics would later associate them with each other. Against this background, Paul's language becomes clearer. Virtually every item in the concrete advice he gives comes from the discussion of the Epicureans. It appears obvious that Paul either thought that the Thessalonians were modeling themselves after the Epicurean fellowships, or that he detected tendencies in them which pointed in that direction, or that they were adopting a similar attitude. It is equally clear that while Paul affirms some things which Christians share with the Epicureans, namely love within the community and a degree of quietism, he departs from them at the crucial point, namely their attitude toward society. Rather than disregard for non-

Christians, Paul seeks approval from the outsiders. The way that approval is to be secured is through economic independence attained by manual labor, a means of support rejected by Epicureans. This means, of course, that Paul shares an ideal with the outsiders, the realization of which would result in the latter's approval. In Paul's thinking the Christian ethic is not always alien to the non-Christian.

This presentation has attempted to signal a change in perception of the social dimension of early Christianity and focused on one aspect of Paul's concerns. My purpose has not been to provide support for any ideology, but simply to provide information and to demonstrate that studying early Christianity from the perspective of social history can be interesting. To do more would require raising questions not appropriate to this context as well as much closer attention to details only touched on in this paper. I should, nevertheless, like to suggest that this approach has value, not only for the historian, but also for the Christian social ethicist and the theologian who are now enabled more readily to discern how theological presuppositions, motives and warrants once functioned and did not function in the thought of the first great Christian theologian.

Chapter 6

The Cultural and Moral Roots of Democratic Capitalism

MICHAEL NOVAK

The question I have been asked to address attempts to articulate some of the moral and religious ideas and values which are implicit in the American system. Why is it that a system like ours needs to be explained? There are only 160 nations in the world, most of them emerging just since World War II and most self-declared socialist nations. There are not more than twenty or thirty which might plausibly be called democratic and capitalist. There is no need to be too abstract about it since the cases are so few. We might as well be quite concrete and try first to understand our own.

The question arises as to why this has not been done over and over. But it has not been. Those who founded, and through experiment developed, this system had just gone through the period of the religious wars. Being practical men they were eager to build a practical system in which it would not be necessary to pass a metaphysical or religious test. You would not have to make a faith commitment at the door in order to enter.

It would be a system in which persons of good will from diverse backgrounds and of diverse faith commitments could nevertheless engage in practical cooperation. I think it was partly for this reason that they were eager not to give too fine a metaphysical cast to what they were doing. That decision, learned through experience, was a sound one and we owe a lot of our success to it.

On the other hand, it has grave deficiencies which have become more and more apparent in each succeeding generation. For one thing, in a world of mass communications the world itself lives more and more by ideas, even bad ideas. It is astonishing how bad ideas have the capacity to win the hearts and allegiance of millions. It is astonishing how entire nations seem to be willing, like the Gadarene swine, to follow crazy ideas over the precipice. And in a world in which ideas are often more powerful than facts, it is a deficiency not to have a theory about oneself. You cannot beat bad ideas with no ideas. Therefore, we take a terrible ideological drubbing in the world when we are unable to defend ourselves intellectually. That is one deficiency.

A second deficiency is low morale here at home. There are many persons working in our system who have no sense of the incredible spiritual beauty of what we are doing, of how rare it is, how original it is, and how important it is for the future of the world. And not having that sense that what they do every day is of spiritual importance, they sell short what they are doing. They are unable to defend it at times before their children who come from the university with questions about what their parents do, questions which their parents sometimes cannot answer. It is not necessarily that the questions are well put, or that the parents think they lack answers, but since they have not read the same books, they do not know how to reply and feel a little less well about themselves. They have been robbed of respect in the eyes of their own children. I think that is a very common experience in the United States.

My father-in-law was a lawyer in Iowa and when I married his daughter I was studying history, philosophy and religion at Harvard. He referred to me, I think with affection, as his son-in-law, the "celestial physicist." He used to make a point of telling me, at least twice a year, "Michael, if you can't do it, teach it." I think that expressed pretty well the way the world used to work. We had the view that if you build a better mousetrap, the world will beat a path to your door. You don't have to argue ideology with the Soviets or with anybody else if you can make an oil drilling bit that can go deeper than theirs. They will come to you. They come for Pepsi-Cola and they come for auto parts.

But practicality is not enough in the sort of world we live in. We are being driven, despite ourselves, to give an account of ourselves, to have a theory about ourselves. I don't think the work of theory has ever been more important.

I want to mention one other aspect of the question before us. There is great praise in all spheres of our lives for the democratic part of our system. Everybody is in favor of that. Even our enemies, who don't mean a thing by it, call themselves democratic societies, a tribute they pay to our ideas. But it is rare to find persons in the intellectual communities of our society, particularly in the humanities or even in the social sciences (apart from economics), who have a word of praise for the capitalist part of our system. That is a most extraordinary thing. I exaggerate only a little if I say that the entire tradition of the humanities for the last two hundred years, in Great Britain and the United States, the two first and most significant capitalist countries, is a tradition of hostility. It is exceedingly difficult to find a single literary figure, a literary critic, a man or woman of letters, a philosopher or a theologian, who has anything but hostility, or at the very most, grudging praise, for the capitalist part of our system.

Some are opposed to capitalism for conservative reasons. They preferred Britain when there were "rose trellises around every rural cottage" — no privies, no floors, but rose trellises. My friend and admired colleague George Will writes his rose trellis column every three months. He describes himself as a "stained glass conservative," anti-capitalist from a conservative point of view. That tradition runs deep among agrarian conservatives and other conservatives in the United States and elsewhere.

Others in the literary tradition are hostile to capitalism from the Left. Their hostility is from the point of view of socialist ideals, sometimes of an authoritarian type, sometimes of a democratic type, but in any case, marked by a vigorous anti-capitalist sentiment.

Consequently, even thinking about the moral or spiritual qualities of capitalism runs headlong into an entire tradition. Paul Tillich, the theologian, describes capitalism as demonic and says that any serious Christian must be a socialist. There was a saying very widely used in Great Britain in the 19th century, that "Christianity is the religion of which socialism is the practice." It would have been shocking to have said then, or to say now, "Christianity is the religion of which capitalism is the practice." That would ring differently upon the ear, and that difference is part of the theme to which I am trying to call attention.

This theme is a largely neglected subject. Once one begins to address it, one finds few guidelines and very little assistance. It seems useful, however, to address the question in the way that Max Weber first posed it in 1904. He wrote two essays about the capitalist spirit and, as he referred to it, the "Protestant ethic." Since he was one of the first social scientists to attempt a planetary view of social systems he raised this question by looking at systems around the world.

The question that interested Weber involved buying and selling, which are immemorial activities. Biblical Jerusalem was a trading capital with no agriculture or industry of note. There is nothing new about buying and selling. Factories are not entirely new. There was shipbuilding in the ancient world and the textile factories of the ninth through the eleventh centuries in Italy and elsewhere. In a word, most of the activities which we link with commerce and industry are not new. Yet there was clearly something new in a few places in Europe, two hundred years ago. Weber was right to say that there was a different spirit. He recognized that something was happening to the human spirit. It's not exactly that there were new ideas afoot, although there were. But there was a new *ethos*, a new set of practices and habits and attitudes expressed increasingly in activities and institutions. They were novel. They were also of enormous power and enormous significance to the future of the human race.

Let's use the date 1776, when Adam Smith wrote *An Inquiry Into the Nature and Causes of the Wealth of Nations*, arguing that

Great Britain should adopt a new system, with a new relation-ship between politics and the economy, rather like the model with which North America (but not South America) was experimenting. That they should be doing something different from what they had been doing was his argument.

At the time he wrote that book, there were approximately 800 million persons in the world. Now there are 4.4 billion. People are not having more babies. Rather, more and more of those children are living and living longer. There has been an enormous transformation in the conditions of life. It has been exactly the sort of transformation that Adam Smith envisioned when he inquired into the causes of wealth, into how we might put a better material base under human beings. At a slightly earlier period, Hobbes once described human life in terms that sound rather like the name of a law firm: Solitary, poor, nasty, brutish, and short. In the year 1800, the average age at death among the oppressed sex in France was 27; of the oppressor sex, 24.

The point which Weber made is that something new hap-pened to the human race, and it happened with extraordinary power and rapidity. It came out of a new spirit and it occurred in very few places. It was different from buying and selling and building factories. Those things had been done without anything like the same effect. That's the way Weber put the question. (While I do not think that Weber's explanation of what that new spirit was, exactly, has survived under examination, I don't mean to go into that inquiry at the moment.)

Let me raise the same kind of question from another point of view. We have thought that the experience begun in this country, like the Lexington "shot heard 'round the world," could be imitated everywhere. We have discovered, especially since World War II, that our system is not easily imitable. We have discovered that it is imitable to some extent in cultures quite different from our own, such as Japan, Hong Kong, Taiwan, South Korea (but not North Korea), in Kenya and other places of the world. In truth, some of these nations have been able to imitate only *part* of our system, the economic, but less so the political part. Although one can give examples, rather more stunning I think, are the multitudes of examples in which our system may have been tried a little, but then the organism seemed to reject it, as the body sometimes rejects a new heart or some other organ.

Therefore, one might imagine the question being posed in this way: What sort of assumptions must there be in a society and what sort of *culture* must there be for the institutions of this democratic *polity*, with its capitalistic *economy*, to take root effectively? We have recently seen Iran reject these, illustrating the reality and the power of cultural presuppositions.

If you put the question this way you begin to see that we take some things for granted. It's easy to do because one's own culture, which doesn't feel like a culture at all, is the hardest thing for one who participates in it to see. It's just reality, just the way things are. When the Peace Corps first sent people overseas they discovered many of the youngsters developed something called "culture shock," a kind of dizziness that overcomes one when what has been taken to be real is not taken very seriously by the people among whom one finds oneself, their sense of reality being different. What the Medievals used to call the "four transcendentals" are of this sort. The beautiful, the real, the good and the true, natural to one's own perception, may not seem to be quite so beautiful or true or good in the perception of others who may look at things a little differently. To have such different perceptions at the very root of one's psyche, at the very root of one's own being, is a shock, a jolt. Even when one overcomes it and learns to adjust and live in a new culture, returning to one's own culture can pose a re-entry problem.

If you try to identify some of the things which we take for granted which make possible a democratic polity in a capitalistic economy, you begin down a road not very well traveled. But it is a road down which many persons, from many points of view, are going to have to go until we come to understand ourselves more directly.

PLURALISM

The first of the underlying values of our culture comes out of the insight I have attempted to build up, namely, the pluralism of our system. The American system is not one system, but three. It is a political system. It is also an economic system.

And it is a moral or cultural system. Each of these systems has its own institutions. In fact, I would even argue that each attracts its own personality type. And these three systems are relatively independent from another, although they are, of course, interdependent also. (My students at Stanford used to tease me, saying that I always did things in threes. I said I couldn't help it. As a Catholic, a trinitarian to the bitter end, it seemed to me perfectly natural that if God is as I think He is, things should come in threes.) In any case, in our system, rather like the Trinity, each of these three is distinct and separate, though together they make one, in a very powerful and important way.

First, let me give an example of dependence. If you make changes in one of these systems, in the political system, or the economic system, or the moral-cultural system, you ordinarily precipitate changes in the other two. For example, if Harvard students graduate and then begin to collect unemployment checks in hardship locations like Aspen and Fort Lauderdale and Paris, they place a burden on the political system and the economic system which these were not intended to bear. These are not underprivileged kids. When I went to Harvard, which was not so very long ago, you could not possibly have done that. You would not have permitted it in yourself, and your friends would have ridiculed you and made you ashamed. But there has been a change in the moral and cultural system, so that one can go on unemployment as a graduate of Harvard in perfectly good conscience. This change in one of the systems has put great pressures on the other two systems, illustrating one small example of their mutual dependence.

As to their independence, let me use one example and you can multiply others at will. I have many friends in the literary and cultural world, and in the world of theology, who cannot interpret the financial pages of the *New York Times* or the *Wall Street Journal*. They do not know what all the symbols mean and they certainly do not know what makes the numbers behave as they do. I'm not sure that anybody knows all of that, but some don't understand even basics of the economic system. More significantly, they live perfectly happy lives. So independent are the systems that it is possible to live in this country and not know or understand the economic system, yet be perfectly content. Similarly, I know people in the business community — not as many, and not as well — but I do know them well enough to know how baffled they are by politicians. They just do not understand how politicians behave. They don't understand how politics works. It's very different from anything they know. And they don't bother to keep up with the intellectuals. They're not terribly impressed by intellectuals, as a matter of fact. Yet again, they live perfectly happy lives.

I also know politicians who, at the top of their form, are very successful. Yet, it seems to be one condition for being a successful politician that one not know anything about the economic system. Nor do political leaders have time to keep up with what the philosophers or the theologians are writing. They don't know what Hans Küng's most recent book is. And they are perfectly happy. Ask a Senator if he likes movies and he says, "Of course." You say, "For example?" and he says, "The Sound of Music." You can live in these three systems and have very little to do with people in the other two.

I don't want to linger too long, and I can't prove this, but I do think that the personality types naturally attracted to each of these systems tend not to like the personality types attracted to the other two. In fact, that seems somehow to be important to the system. The founding fathers, the inventors of our system, wanted to fragment power. The one thing they feared most was the will-to-power. They didn't want to repress it (what a dreadfully boring and stagnant civilization would result from any attempt to repress the will to power), but to fragment it. Almost all societies in history were unitary societies in which one class of persons came to power at the top, as the clergy in Iran today. In other countries it was the police or the military. In still other countries it was the aristocracy or landowners. In such societies one class tends to make all the decisions — political, economic and religious.

Our founding fathers wanted a system in which decisions would be made by different people in separate institutions. They wanted a system in which the will to power would work in such a fashion that the most talented people in each one of these sets of institutions, when they came to the top of their particular system, would discover that they were not "king" of the entire mountain since they would understand only how one system works but not the other two.

It's a very rare person in America who understands even two of these systems. It's hard enough to understand how one of them works. To give you an example, it's exceedingly difficult to understand what makes an idea work in America. Of all the multiplicity of ideas, why are some believed so readily? How does one of them come to have so much influence in society in such a short period of time? What are the processes by which ideas find their way through our society? It's a very tricky question. I think it can be answered, but it's not easy to answer.

And if it's hard to understand the moral-cultural system, it's equally hard to understand how things work in the economic system and the political system.

Now, I would be willing to grant that our political scientists have given us a reasonable understanding of how the political system works, and our economists a reasonable understanding (I'm a little more doubtful there) of how the economic system works. However, we humanists have done a deplorable job in describing the way the moral-cultural system works.

To illustrate our ignorance of the geography of the American spirit, how do you explain the fact that so many first rate journalists were at such a loss when Jimmy Carter was running for the Presidency, and described for the first time in North Carolina (and not there by accident, I think) that he was a "born-again Christian?" They immediately jumped to the telephone and ran to an encyclopedia trying to find out what it is to be a born-again Christian. Now, how can you be a well-educated American and not know what is meant by "born again," an experience known to perhaps 50 million of your fellow citizens? Yet it is perfectly possible today to go to Harvard or Yale or Princeton and not know what it is to be born again. That is to say, it's possible to be ignorant about the spiritual geography of a great many of one's fellow citizens. That is a failing of the humanist. We have failed to draw maps of our own territory. We have worked our own parochial shores but we don't have a good understanding of the range of our country's whole moral-cultural system and its institutions.

Nobody that I know has put together all three of these things. There is not one single book that I know of that I could put in the hands of graduate students, or in the hands of a journalist from Italy or France or Germany and say, "This is the way the American system, in its three parts, works. This is the way the economy works with the politics and with the moral-cultural system," for instance. That book does not exist.

This, then, is the first point that I would like to establish (although I realize I'm only hinting at these things rather than really establishing them). One of the great contributions of our society has been its fundamental institutional and structural pluralism. It is a separation of systems with still further separations within each system: within the political system, the separation of powers; within the economic system, the separation of labor and management and the separation of economic regions with their different economic interests. Even industries are quite different from one another in their needs, their purposes, and their interests. It is a pluralism which keeps being magnified throughout the system with boxes within boxes within boxes.

COMMUNITY

The second of these powerful moral-cultural ideas which I want to draw on (you won't be surprised to learn there are three) is community. Our sort of society depends absolutely on certain understandings about community. I believe that our society is as communal as any society ever was, though in a very different and unique way. The original shape of our sense of community is so unique that it often baffles those who try to describe us. We are frequently described as individualists — as "Marlboro men." But it's not true. My eight-year-old daughter already belongs to more organizations and associations than my wife and I together can drive her to. And we want it that way. We want our children to belong to multiple groups, to belong to very different sorts of associations, able to move in and out of various groups freely, openly and easily. We want them, for example, to be able when they are old enough to show up in a state like New Hampshire every four years, join with groups of strangers who have never met before, and without anybody giving them orders, organize overnight a campaign in an entire state. This capacity of 18, 19, and 20 year old youngsters, so inured to the teamwork and cooperation of working with others, comes naturally, without anybody giving them orders about what to do. It is an extraordinary achievement of community in a people.

There are some aspects of community under capitalism which I would like to stress because they are so often ignored. First, it is significant that Adam Smith called his book *An Inquiry Into the Nature and the Causes of the Wealth of Nations* — not of individuals, not even of Scotland, for which he had a fierce love (he knew quite well the difference between Scotland and Britain). But the fundamental intention of this system for whose coming into being he was arguing is the wealth of *all* nations. The fundamental intention of this system, of which we are a part, aims at all humanity. Its purposes will not be achieved until a material base has been placed under all of humanity. In fact, the larger part of his book is about parts of the world which we now refer to as the "Third World." This system was never designed merely for individuals growing wealthy in their individuality.

Second, the great social invention of this system, it turns out, was the corporation, not the individual. The basic insight was that the economic task is far more complicated than any one person can perform. Further, its character is more enduring than any one generation. A form of organization was needed which would allow many people to cooperate across time and space, over periods of time longer than the single generation in which the corporation was first invented. Almost by accident, and by slow experiment, the corporation developed. In 1800, as Oscar Handlin has shown, there were more corporations in the United States alone than in all of Europe combined. There were relatively few lawyers and almost no corporation law, thus nobody knew what you could not do. If you wanted to start a corporation, you just started it. You attacked a a job and you did it. Corporations in Great Britain at that time were still largely grants from the crown. You can still see on some British products, "By order of or by favor of her majesty." In England corporations were privileges granted to few people. But this was not so in the United States. It was sufficient merely for several people to cooperate in attacking a task that one alone could not attack, in order to launch a corporation and to register it with the government under restrictions or regulations that gradually became more complex.

The third point about the kind of community experienced in the United States is that it is quite different from that experienced in other cultures. May its most visible force can be seen by comparing it with the sort of community known to our grandparents. Mine, in their little village in the mountains of Slovakia in the center of Europe, could work in the fields within sound of the bells of the parish church. They could work in a way which would have seemed almost unchanged over a thousand years. They would see very few others from beyond their own valley. The values and the traditions of the church, and perhaps of the castle down in the valley which was the symbol of the political system of that place, had been relatively unchanged for very long periods of time. And, it was quite integrated. The union of church and state and culture was a seamless garment.

Now imagine growing up in a village where one's brothers and sisters and cousins held the same views. And imagine how much everybody knew about everybody else, and how difficult it was to break away from the community. That is a community of a very powerful sort. While it is attractive on the one hand, it is quite oppressive and quite stifling if looked at from another point of view. Compare that with the sort of community shared by my brothers and sisters two generations later in the United States. It's a radically different kind of life. Yet I would not say it is lacking in community. At least I do not experience it that way.

I cherish the sort of communities that we have in the United States, with freedom of moving in and out of them, because the emphasis is on colleagueship rather than village life, as the basic model of community. At the American Enterprise Institute, for instance, I see as powerful a form of community as I have ever seen. There, a group of scholars who don't spend a great deal of time looking into one another's eyes or cultivating warm feelings towards one another, are instead engaged upon a common task. They enjoy one another's company, respect one another, and deal fairly, honestly and courteously with one another. It's a marvelous form of community — to go through battles together, to endure bad times and good times together. It is different from the image of the Medieval village which dominates so much of our writing about community. Yet this colleagueship is an important community of consent, of contract, and of choice. And that's what is extraordinarily good about it.

As we all know, of course, having lived for awhile, we can overestimate some things. We may not choose this colleague-ship as much as we find our way into it by accident and by hazard. We make a choice, but it is also not by choice.

What I want to say is that there are mysteries of community which we have not pierced. We have been too influenced by a model we borrowed from Europe. I notice in arguments with European colleagues that there is too much concern with two polar concepts only: the individual on the one hand and the collective on the other hand, without the insight that neither one of those concepts expresses the American form of life. The American form is extraordinarily associative. We are joiners. We are belongers. We are much closer to our families and to our various sorts of communities than we commonly think, though not close in the sense in which collectives are close.

The rare, ornery, sharp-edged individual is getting more rare among us. There were more such obstreperous persons in my grandparents' generation than in ours. A friend of mine from Italy pointed out to me that he wouldn't like to live here because Americans not only work forty hours in a week, but spend another forty hours when they get home going to Boy Scout meetings, church meetings, and the PTA. They are meeting-goers. He said, "You work eighty hours a week including forty hours in various voluntary associations!"

Finally, I would like to talk about the importance of our conception of sin. I mentioned earlier that one of the things that preoccupied the founders of our system was the danger of power and of tyranny. They wrote a lot about their fear of tyranny. While they believed that most human beings, most of the time, are capable of a certain decency, a certain compassion, a certain law-abidingness (humans are not depraved), never-theless, all human beings, some of the time, are not to be trusted. They embossed this wisdom on our coins. You can't trust a President so you have a Congress. But you can't trust a Congress so you have two of them. And you can't trust either House of Congress so you have judges. And you can't trust judges, so you appoint some and elect some. Then, with all of those you have the people. But you can't trust the people directly, except in a referendum. Even when you go directly to the people, it is not very often and only under certain conditions. Most of your reliance on the people is by way of a constituted majority because you do not trust a numerical majority. You work instead through representative majorities, which is quite a different concept. The founders summed up all this wisdom in the little slogan they embossed on our coins: "In God we trust," which as we Catholics interpret it, means "nobody else."

This idea had direct theological expression. But quite obviously, it was also a perfectly secular experience. It came from sheer observation of matters of fact and probability. Human beings tend to abuse power. Even the best human beings cannot be trusted with power. Therefore, you fragment and divide powers to provide checks and balances and to create space between them.

The last point I would like to mention is one we most commonly overlook. It is that in order to defeat sin and turn it to advantage, it is important to promote commerce and industry. This practical insight grew out of the experience of the free cities. The European cities grew up as markets. "City air breathes free," the slogan was, "City air makes free." And this freedom, based in part on the growth of commerce and industry, destroys the relationship between the lords and the serfs, giving a middle ground for producing persons who are neither lords nor serfs.

This insight was picked up by our founding fathers. Commerce and industry have certain characteristics attached to them which are fruitful for democracies and for the development of the human spirit. People of commerce are not so high as the aristocracy, nor so idealistic and lofty as religious aspiration would commend. But if you must make a choice of building a society around an aristocracy, or building a society around the clergy, or building a society around persons of commerce and industry, which will be more useful for democracy? Which will be more useful for economic prosperity? And which, at least indirectly, will be more fruitful for the Holy Spirit and for the human spirit?

The founders of our society argued that commerce and industry are the best bet. Compare them with the alternatives, and test the fruit. They have these qualities: they favor a character or person who is non-heroic, given to attending to small savings and small gains. This person is a moderate, with reasonable expectations of human behavior. He has an interest in law-abidingness because persons of commerce and industry must make contracts which will not be fulfilled for some time, often for years. They must depend upon a stable system of laws for the fulfillment of those contracts and commitments. They have an interest in peace for the very same reason. War, revolution, and disruption are extremely damaging to their interests.

And, finally, they have the most serious interest of anybody in interdependence. A world built on commerce, on trade and on industry, the founders argued, would become an interdependent world. It would lose a lot, for a world built around persons of commerce and industry would not have quite the verve or flash as a world built around aristocrats. It would not have quite the pretensions to holiness as a world built around the clergy. It would not have the spirit of martial adventure of a society build around the military. But for purposes of democracy and prosperity, it would serve more people, especially the poor, better than any other system.

This, as they pointed out, was a very humble wisdom. Instead of looking for utopia, one lowers one's eyes to what can, with effort, be done. And this, they argued, was in the classic Jewish and Christian spirit. This is exactly the characteristic mode of both Judaism and Christianity. While it might be taken on entirely secular gounds, it is entirely consistent with the sort of religious nourishment which our culture has been undergoing for some 3,000 years.

Chapter 7

Another Source of the Wealth of Nations

GEORGE GILDER

Upon my recent return from Britain (where I spent the summer doing an "English edition" of *Wealth and Poverty*) I was shocked and perplexed by the scene that confronted me on the newstands. Everywhere I looked there were newspaper headlines, and magazine features talking of collapsing markets and soaring interest rates. It seemed to me impossible that this could be the United States. I wondered if the air traffic controllers had dispatched me back to London where I had become familiar with such depressing reading.

I really should not have been surprised, however. In February of this year, working on the economic policy statement of the President, I had found the entire Office of Management and Budget (OMB) plunged in gloom as they contemplated the economic situation bequeathed by the previous Administration. They were predicting exactly our current plight: a credit crunch which would result in very high interest rates and would jeopardize the early phases of the President's program. Indeed, OMB Director David Stockman and Congressman Jack Kemp had issued the famous "Dunkirk Manifesto" that itself prophesied precisely the kind of developments we are now seeing — unless the President could declare a national economic emergency and reduce the 1981 Carter budget as well as later budgets. So I should not have been surprised.

What in fact we've experienced during the last year is a continuation of past policies: a further increase in federal spending and a continuation of President Carter's efforts to balance the budget by raising taxes. Indeed, over the last year, although there has been a great deal of talk about tax cuts, what has actually occurred is another long period of bracket creep with a ten percent rise in most people's tax rates. Thus we have had another tax increase prompted by the anticipation of expanding deficits. I think this is really the crux of the problem. Under the Carter administration, the deficit was quite successfully controlled. They reduced it from something like 4 percent of GNP to just over one percent, but interest rates did not respond very well; they nearly doubled. Inflation was not brought to a halt; as a matter of fact, we precipitated the very configuration of crises that we currently confront.

Although I should not have been surprised by the condition of the economy when I returned, I was completely justified in my shock at the continued incomprehension of supply-side economics that I saw in all media coverage of the tax cut, of the deficit, and of Reagan's policies. For example, there continued the complete breakdown of communication between the front page of the *Wall Street Journal* and the editorial page. These people never talk to one another. So we continued to find the tax cut defined as a $552 billion reduction, as if the government would necessarily have received $552 billion in additional revenues if it had not enacted the cut. But this assumption assumes that revenues would have continued to increase if we allowed a 46 percent increase in marginal tax rates over the next four or five years. Those who believe that the government would have actually collected this $552 billion in additional revenue, in a time when taxes continue to rise at that pace, demonstrate a complete ignorance of the empirical argument which supply-side economists have expounded. They show that they do not comprehend what has been happening during the previous decade when this method of controlling inflation was continually in effect.

People talk about supply-side economics as being "a big riverboat gamble, an untested theory." Well, one theory has been very fully tested and that is the theory that by raising taxes you can control inflation. We've been raising taxes 80 percent faster than the price level for a decade. It's hard to understand how further increases in taxes are likely to control inflation, and I'm convinced that they won't. What happens is that when taxes go up, savings go down. Even if the deficit diminishes, the burden of the deficit on total national savings increases, which is what happened under President Carter.

Carter reduced the deficit brilliantly. But at the same time he virtually extinguished personal savings in America, which, by the end of 1979 had reached 3.6 percent. What matters is not the relationship of the deficit to gross national product. What matters is the relationship of the deficit to total national savings, because it's the savings that finance the deficit. If you raise taxes and thus reduce savings, even a smaller deficit will exert greater inflationary pressures on the Federal Reserve to monetize it. Tax increases now will not work and can't work. We have to continue on our current course.

Incidentally, I saw yesterday a very interesting little oversight in the pages of the *Wall Street Journal*. This was an article on Austria by Lindsey Clark, another of the repeated stories in various newspapers on the Austrian miracle. Congressional Joint Economic Committee Chairman Henry Reuss did a brief essay in the *Washington Post* to demonstrate that the Austrian experience shows the utter futility of supply-side economics. None of these stories which focus on the low inflation, low interest rates, large money growth and substantial deficits of Austria, mention that between 1973 and 1976 the Austrians cut their marginal tax rates by 33 percent. Austria is a very good example of the anti-inflationary impact of substantial cuts in marginal tax rates.

So, there continues to be a resistance to recognizing the key role of taxation in destroying incentives and causing inflation. There's still the idea that somehow we can reduce the deficit by increasing taxation, and thus generate an economic expansion.

But I don't chiefly want to discuss the details of supply-side economics today. More important is understanding that the concept of capitalism which underlies most analyses of how capitalism works, including a considerable amount of supply-side analysis, is erroneous. The supply-siders often imply, as do the Keynesians and most other analysts, that capitalism works because it's a particularly ingenious system of incentives, that it offers rewards for productive activity and thus induces it —that capitalism is somehow successful because it's an extraordinarily ingenious and tantalizing arrangement of carrots and sticks — that self-interest and the desire to consume comprise the driving force of the capitalist system.

I think this concept is misconceived. The extent of the misconception, which also underlies the prevailing low estimates of the impact of tax cuts on economic activity, became increasingly clear to me as I wrote and then published *Wealth and Poverty*. While writing the book, I interviewed businessmen. (This was one of the reasons *Wealth and Poverty* was different and perhaps more useful than some other books on economics. I didn't consult observers of the economy; I chiefly consulted the makers of it.) During the course of all these interviews, I got a fairly acute sense of where the best opportunities for investment were in the U.S. economy, where I could best devote any energies and monies that I might acquire. At the time, I didn't have any money so I couldn't make any investments. But I expected that someday when I did make some investments, I could benefit from the great knowledge that I had acquired about opportunities in the U.S. economy during the course of researching *Wealth and Poverty*.

What happened after I actually did get some money (and this fact was widely publicized) was quite surprising. It immediately became clear that I wasn't going to be permitted to use my own knowledge to make productive investments in the U.S. economy. Now that I *had* some money, I wasn't going to be allowed to invest it usefully. I wasn't going to be allowed to use the knowledge that I had acquired during the course of my writings at all. Instead I was supposed to consult with tax consultants, tax accountants, tax planners, deal makers of every description, people telling me about the necessity of diverting funds to the Cayman Islands and from there to Curacao. There was the need to invest in these extraordinarily intricate 1031 real estate swaps and triple-net real estate leases. All these extraordinarily complex kinds of activities have at least one thing in common: they are virtually all unproductive in character.

This is what high tax rates do to virtually anybody who

makes money in America. The rates are not merely destroying incentives. Perhaps their crucial role is in destroying morale and knowledge. The crucial capital in any capitalist system is not physical. It's not natural resources, or even plant and equipment; it's the ever increasing fund of metaphysical capital: comprising a combination of knowledge, faith, courage, and the crucial human characteristics of capitalist entrepreneurs.

To understand how this works, you first have to comprehend that capitalist investments are essentially experiments. There are sixteen-million small businesses in America today and these small businesses are laboratory tests of entrepreneurial ideas. When a small business succeeds, it generates not just profit. It doesn't just confer a greater ability to consume on the owner of the business. It also creates knowledge, which confers a greater ability to invest productively.

So there's a yield of profit and a yield of knowledge. The reason capitalism succeeds is because it links the growth of knowledge with an increase in power. The profit confers power; the experiment confers knowledge. The knowledge generated by the entrepreneurial experiment improves the process of investment, and thus generates new metaphysical capital that makes the economy work. This is the crux of capitalist growth. It's not that the profit acts as an overwhelming incentive to the businessman. It's that the profit infuses the knowledge he gains with the power to control the future course of investments.

The businessman doesn't have to resort to some government bureaucracy to gain permission and resources to continue to exploit his ideas. Rather, the capitalist system assigns to the very same people who forgo short term gratification, who forgo immediate desires to consume, the power to control the future course of investments. This is the key to capitalist success. The best investors are the people who are most willing to eschew immediate gratifications in pursuit of long-term goals and thus have the power to control the future of the economy. High tax rates destroy this link between knowledge and power. The knowledge increases, but rather than being used to control the future course of investments, it's dismissed in favor of the unproductive knowledge of lawyers and tax consultants and tax analysts of various kinds.

This is the essential process of capitalist growth. Businessmen are not greedier consumers than other people. The fact is that they have more money because money is their very means of production. Money is crucial to the performance of their entrepreneurial role.

Just as a professor of sociology or science needs tenure and summer vacations and research assistants and sabbaticals and beautiful green campuses and also independence and freedom to pursue his own ideas, so the businessman needs to have access to financial resources to perform his role in the economy. He is not chiefly motivated by the desire to consume. He is the person who's willing to defer consumption and save. That's what characterizes his nature. As establishment economists are increasingly coming to understand in their rejection of the "life-cycle" theory of savings, capitalists do not chiefly save for their own retirement; their savings follow not their own life cycle but a cycle of generations, as they build up the capital of the country and defer and diffuse consumption not merely to their own children and grandchildren but to the entire society.

The businessmen who are really devoted to their businesses, who make the most important contributions to society, who explain the secret of capitalist success, are not big hoarders and consumers. They are people who are continually reinvesting in the system. They are continually giving back, continually refraining from consumption, and continuing to save and invest in the future of the economy.

How arose this misconception of the way capitalism works? How did the basic demand side idea — that humans are chiefly consumers rather than builders and creators — get entrenched as the prevailing psychological theory of capitalism. Where did we get the idea that the desire for self-indulgence is what chiefly motivates the producers of the system? I am afraid I think it began with the greatest theorist of capitalism, Adam Smith.

Adam Smith was a great intellectual. Intellectuals in general have tended throughout history to disdain people "in trade." They always seek some explanation of the success of capitalism that does not entail praising the superior qualities of business-men. So what has emerged is a kind of "businessmen are bastards" theory, which one finds among conservatives virtually as much as among liberals. Adam Smith evinced it to the most striking degree throughout the pages of both *The Theory of*

Moral Sentiments and *The Wealth of Nations*. Both books are replete with denunciations of the character of businessmen. In an apparent effort to dramatize his miraculous theory of the market, which transmutes these "voracious drives," "vain indulgences" and "compulsive ambitions" into a steadily growing and expanding economy, Smith really lets himself go. These pejoratives applied to business are quite extraordinary in a man who has the reputation today as being one of the great defenders of business.

The problem began because in his analysis, Adam Smith focused not on the creative activities of businessmen as the source of the growth of capitalism, but rather on the freedom of markets. Today you find most conservative economists stress free markets rather than private enterprise and capitalism as the source of economic growth. The ultimate example of this sort of misunderstanding comes from Adam Smith's assertion that division of labor is determined by the extent of the market, as if somehow the market itself evokes from these greedy and doltish businessmen the kind of creativity that we find manifested in capitalist economies.

Now, free markets are absolutely indispensable to capitalism. But to focus on exchange as the crux of capitalist growth, to focus on market transactions as the epitome of capitalism, is diversionary. Of course, market transactions do represent very calculated acts of self-interest which might be described as narrow self-interest. They are a calculation of value. But the source of capitalist growth is not found in market exchanges. Rather it is found in the preceding initiatives — the creative, originating initiatives of entrepreneurs. In other words, supply precedes demand. The transactions of demand in the marketplace are preceded by the feats of entrepreneurs.

For some time I have been describing investments as analogous to gifts. During the course of writing other books I read a great deal of anthropology. One of the things I noticed throughout these works was a great preoccupation with gift-giving. Claude Levi Strauss has described gift-giving as fundamental to all human societies: in *The Essay on The Gift*, Marcel Mauss, another leading French anthropologist, also has remarked on the ubiquity of gift-giving in primitive societies. Other anthropologists have noticed this phenomenon, and many of them say, "Isn't it too bad that in contemporary society you don't find this gift-giving? Instead what we have is these impersonal marketplace exchanges which cause alienation and demoralization; the economic process has been dehumanized by the eclipse of the giving impulse under capitalism." The problem of Marcel Mauss and Levi Strauss is the same as the problem of Adam Smith and his analysis. He focuses on the denouement of the economic process, the final buying and selling, rather than on the preceding activities — original, creative activities of entrepreneurs.

When you contemplate what capitalists do you can see how capitalist investments and the launching of new businesses constitute a pattern of giving which is more ambitious and far-reaching than any simple offering that one finds in primitive societies. As a matter of fact, I see the prevalence of gift-giving in primitive societies is evidence that capitalism is fundamental to all human life and wealth creation. But the giving process has found its fruition in contemporary capitalism. What a businessman does is give of his wealth, his work, his energies, long before any return is specified. A gift isn't defined by the complete absence of any return. In these primitive societies reciprocation was very much expected. A gift is defined by the absence of a pre-determined return. Consider what a businessman does. He assembles his wealth, he devotes his work to figuring out an opportunity in marketplace, he invents or designs goods and services, he figures out how to produce them, he hires people, he rents buildings, he purchases equipment, he piles up inventory; he follows a long process which often exhausts him of both his finances and his energies before he has even a clue to a return. This is the crucial process of capitalism. It is a process of giving long before any return is assured.

As a matter of fact, many of these processes of giving are aborted long before any business is launched. Two-thirds of all American businesses fail within five years. The vast majority of inventions are never exploited at all. In the book business (which I know well), there are hundreds of books written for every one that makes any kind of profit at all, and the writing of a book is an entrepreneurial venture for most people. Most people do not get advances. I never used to take advances because I always assumed my book would be worth more after I wrote it than beforehand, which turned out to be true in only one case.

The point is that what makes capitalism go in these sixteen-million small businesses that provide the creative ferment in the system, is the continuing gifts of entrepreneurs — of their work and wealth — without any predetermined return. That is the crucial process of capitalist growth. It is not a process of very calculating markets and short-term analysis. It is a process that is dependent on faith in the future because these long-term business investments cannot be proven promising beforehand. There is no way to predict whether these investments will succeed. As a matter of fact, any rational calculation would predict their failure most of the time. In fact, if you consult the leading experts in most areas, they always will predict the failure of a new venture based on an original idea.

For example, I recently read a book by John Masters, a natural gas geologist who came from Texas and is head of Canadian Hunter Corporation. Canadian Hunter Corporation has recently discovered an estimated 440-trillion cubic feet of natural gas, enough to fuel America well into the 21st century. This may not all be proven economic, but nonetheless, he found vast quantities of natural gas. The theory that he employed was also extended to the United States and facilitated the discoveries in the Overthrust Belt in the Rockies.

The crucial point in this theory is that Masters was not an oil or gas geologist originally. He was not a recognized expert in the field; he was a uranium specialist working for Kerr-McGee, who previously had made the biggest discovery of uranium in America, called Ambrosia Lake in Utah. He concluded, in a novel geological theory, that there was a huge basin of natural gas in Western Canada in areas that had already been heavily explored by all the major oil companies. So he went north to prove his theory. He went to every major oil company for support, and, of course, none would grant him any. All leading geologists said he was crazy, and all the regnant expertise in the field predicted his failure.

Masters finally got his capital not from an oil or gas company at all, but from a copper company. The copper company didn't know enough about natural gas to see that he was a kook — to perceive the impossibility of finding fuel in Western Canada in areas which had been thoroughly explored. Well, Masters bought up all the leases in Western Canada very cheaply because it had been explored already, and the discoveries that he made have now led to a frantic attempt to buy back into this region by all of the oil companies that had rejected him. The discoveries probably portend the end of the energy crisis through the use of the cleanest and most efficient of all fuels, natural gas.

The moral of this story is that the kind of commitment and faith that somebody like him displays, which goes far beyond any narrow calculations of self-interest or any easy analysis by experts, is crucial to all major breakthroughs. They always defy the conventions of expertise to which any government planner will necessarily defer. For example, the application of alternating current was denounced by Thomas Edison. Here was the greatest expert in the history of electricity, who toward the end of his life devoted most of his time to an effort to suppress alternating current. He said it was dangerous, perilous, and erratic and posed terrible problems for the future. If you had a planned economy where the government deferred to expertise, alternating current would have been suppressed by Thomas Edison. But we had a free economy which allowed it to succeed.

The point is that an impulse of giving is the crux of capitalist success. It is an outgoing impulse, not a narrow matter of calculated self-interest. I believe that our real problem now is the eclipse of this giving impulse, with its essentially moral basis, by the increasing prevalence of narrow self-interest. I think narrow self-interest leads, as by an invisible hand, to an ever-growing welfare state, because people pursuing self-interest will chiefly want comfort and security. They want an assured pattern of future consumption and that can best be offered by government through an expansion of the welfare state.

I think, moreover, that the essential moral and religious foundations of capitalism, which manifest themselves in a giving and generous spirit, depend for their success on sensitivity to the needs of others. The success of these business experiments depends on whether they respond to the needs of others, and whether or not others succeed. Contrary to the sort of zero-sum game analysis, capitalism is dependent upon the successes of others.

The best development in the world economy in recent years has been the emergence of Japan — the triumph of capitalism in Asia. That's not a threat to us; it probably made possible the triumph of the Reagan revolution in the United States. It was the demonstrated success of capitalism in Japan that made it so difficult for people to claim that high taxes and government control was a way to achieve economic success in the United States. One of my chief irritations when I came back to America was to read endless analyses of the Japanese economy suggesting that it is a triumph of socialism and government management in some way. In fact, the Japanese have almost twice as many small businesses per capita as we do. Over half of their employment is provided by businesses employing less than 50 people (compared to about 25 percent of our employment). They probably have a more dynamic and entrepreneurial system than we do.

In explaining the Japanese success, the media have focused on the Ministry of Trade and Industry (MITI), the Japanese government planning agency which essentially offers predictions about the economy and tries to persuade businesses to defer to the plan. Yet their major proposal in the 1960's was that the Japanese get out of the auto business. More specifically they resisted the entry of all these motorcycle companies into the car business because it was obvious to them that Honda, for example, could not make a salable automobile. They were motorcycle makers and they should not try to make automobiles.

The fact is that the greatest successes in the Japanese economy have not been sponsored by government at all. They have been entrepreneurial companies like Sony, which grew without any government aid from a small maker of electric coffee pots in a warehouse after the Second World War. Incidentally, Sony's leaders are prime advocates of supply-side economics. They say the crucial thing in their company's growth was their refusal to pay any attention to market surveys. They defy market surveys. They understand that there is no demand for new products, and that if you have an economy that is based on market demand, you necessarily have a stagnant economy. It is the new products, the surprising new ventures that galvanize new demand and generate economic growth. Thus, it is these new ideas which emerge from this process of giving without a predetermined return which is the foundation of capitalism.

There is a great effort among the defenders of capitalism to defer to a sort of scientific mentality, that capitalism really operates according to a science. It is based on these optimizing consumers, on this calculable computation of self-interest, which is very attractive to economists. But I do not think it is the best way to defend capitalism, nor do I think it persuades people in the first place to say that businessmen are bastards and the best thing to do is let them loose and may the best bastard win. That is not a plausible theory of capitalism. It is rejected by most religious leaders and it is wrong. The crucial change which I hope to see on the right in coming years is that they learn how to see the real sources and benefits of capitalist growth, and stop trying to explain away the success of capitalism as a mere manifestation of an intricate interplay of human greed. I also hope that American leaders will show less credence in the narrow computations of budgetary expertise and more faith in the creativity of unleashed entrepreneurs.

Chapter 8

Law and Economics: An Interdisciplinary Approach That Works

HENRY G. MANNE

O ne of the few concepts clearly shared be economists and lawyers is that each party who knowingly enters a contract will be made better off thereby. Economists refer to this notion as "mutual gains from trade," while lawyers illustrate the point by doctrines such as consideration or mutuality. Any of these notions, including that beleaguered subcategory of contract called marriage, serves as a nice metaphor for describing the emerging field of law and economics. For historically law and economics each suffered distinctive intellectual weaknesses which, almost miraculously, the other could remedy.

To understand the complex development of the combined field of law and economics it is important to know something of the intellectual history of each of the separate fields. Only then can the benefits from any intellectual exchange be clearly understood.

We start with 19th century American law and jurisprudence. Here, with the simplifying lens of history to aid us, we will characterize our legal system as being dominated by the style of common-law adjudication. Austinian jurisprudence, with its sometimes simplistic notion of precedent magically resolving all issues, dominated the thinking of practicing lawyers, judges, and law professors. While there were certain exceptions, for the most part law was thought of as appellate case law, and the style was not profoundly different from that which common law courts had used for four hundred years.

Blackstone's notion that there was a kind of natural order embodied in the common law (presumably including the common law process and not merely a body of rules that could be stated at one moment in time) comforted legal thinkers for 150 years, right into the 20th century. This system of case law reasoning idealized by Blackstone and later giants of law seems strangely unscientific, almost to the point of superstition, to modern observers. For example, judges and lawyers were not supposed to consider the economic impact of the holding of a given case nor the redistributional or social consequences that might follow one holding or another. Such thoughts would rarely enter the head of a lawyer, a judge, or a law professor in, say, 1870. And if such a thought did occur and might conceivably influence an argument or a holding, it would have to be handled in the most subtle and subliminal fashion. The answer to all issues that reached courts or academic consideration were to be sought in that brooding omnipresence known as the common law.

This mental set about law was further strengthened by the nature of litigants and the kinds of issues they raised. Only rarely, and then most often on some frontier of constitutional law and political activity, would a case have obvious significance for a large number of individuals. Facts like those in *Plessy vs. Ferguson* were still exceptional in litigation and not, as is true today, commonplace. Furthermore, the great volume of civil litigation involved claims by one individual or firm against another. The phrase "administrative law" was not yet thought even to have a place in American law. The type of cases that judges and law professors were asked to address put little pressure on the system to develop a new jurisprudence.

All this began to change in the last part of the first quarter of the 20th century. Beginning with Roscoe Pound, if not with Oliver Wendell Holmes, the group who later came to be known as American Legal Realists began their sharp and telling criticism of Austinian jurisprudence and 19th century legal style. The Legal Realists pointed with great effect to the intellectual vacuousness of a pure common-law jurisprudence. It had been a mistake, they claimed, on the part of Blackstone and other legal philosophers to think of the common law as being scientific merely because it offered an extensive classification system. It offered no answers that could be tested by objective standards, and therefore it lacked scientific validity. The realists may have taken the common lawyers claims to disinterest too seriously, but they demanded more convincing rationalizations for legal holdings than that they were based on earlier precedents.

Later Legal Realists attempted to offer an affirmative theory of legal development. Some based their ideas on sociology, some on psychoanalytical theory, and still others on Marxian views of a class struggle. Alas, none succeeded in offering an intellectually respectable scheme to replace the theory as well as the procedures and techniques the law had developed. The Legal Realists did succeed in destroying much myth about our legal system, but in the end they can only be credited as successful iconoclasts. They never built anything new to replace the views of earlier legal philosophers.

While the Legal Realists can be said to have paved the way for a later joining of law and objective social science, it is likely that exogenous changes outside of courtrooms and law professors' offices had far more effect on our jurisprudence. While decisions in traditional common-law cases brought by private litigants showed little concern for the social welfare implications of holdings, changes in the subject matter of lawsuits early in the century did reflect the newer concerns.

First, the growth of administrative law at all levels of government immediately confronted judges and, therefore, law professors with issues that could rarely be treated with precedent. The very subject matter and the very nature of administrative regulation dictated that anyone concerned with the law address substantive economic and other policy issues. Rate regulations, safety rules, trade regulation, zoning, and myriad other topics forced courts at least partially into the mold of administrators. And while much of administrative law has of necessity taken on procedural coloration, the substantive issues are never far below the surface and very frequently are the focus of litigation.

Administratrive law was not the only body of law that pushed courts away from a traditional view of litigation. In some areas like antitrust law, the legal standard that courts were to apply was actually stated in economic terms. In such areas a judge was to a considerable degree invited to address each case as a new issue to test whether it conformed to the economic standard. Obviously, in such a field of statutory development, precedent could never have quite the strength that it did in the common-law fields. So it was in many other areas of law as well, including pricing regulations, income tax, labor relations, employment discrimination, etc. Only the most unimaginative participants in the legal process could fail to realize that judges (and, willy-nilly law professors) would have to look elsewhere for answers to such problems. Legal writing, and to some extent judicial opinions, tended more and more to sound like ideological tracts with results determined by some superficial and simplistic moralizing. Clearly this state of affairs, though it is still the dominant mode in legal literature, would have to give way eventually to a more analytical and persuasive style of exposition.

We must note here, too, another influence on 20th century law; that is the much expanded use of lawyers to staff important policy making positions in government, not merely in legislatures but in the mushrooming administrative area of government. Naturally this has generated an increased use of lawyers in private enterprise to deal with their counterparts in government. And as this professional evolution occurred, it became clear for still another reason that traditional legal education suffered serious gaps which only a familiarity with the policy sciences could correct.

The problems of economic science were of a quite different nature from those of law. Economists in the dominant neoclassical tradition had, by the turn of the century, a fairly well developed theoretical apparatus for simulating and analyzing real world problems. And the 20th century was to see the development of even more sophisticated and useful theoretical models.

The major difficulty with economics was that the shortcomings of purely theoretical structures in explaining real world events were little noted by economic practitioners. Indeed they came in a sense to believe that their theory was actually a description of reality, and their conception of the real world was formed more by the theories they had to work with than it was by any objective scientific measure of phenomena.

The major critics of the static neoclassical models were not, as in the case of the Legal Realists, merely iconoclasts. Indeed the early great critics of static neoclassical models, men like Schumpeter, von Mises, Hayek, and Knight also made some of the most important advances in theory. To some extent, however, their implicit criticism of the earlier paradigm did have some of the same effect as did the Legal Realists' purely negative criticism. It turned the main body of academic economists away from the strong foundations of neoclassical theory as well as from its weaknesses.

This intellectual shift away from more individualistic concerns was bolstered considerably by the advent of the great depression and the appearance in 1936 of John Maynard Keynes' *The General Theory of Employment Interest and Money.* These two events were sufficient to deflect the major attention of economists from the theory of markets, prices, efficient allocation of resources and the theory of the firm into issues of deflation, deficit spending, fiscal and monetary policy, aggregate demand, employment levels, and gross national product. There was little in this development that could ever impact significantly on law or legal philosophy. The same was *a fortiori* true of mathematical economics that began to flourish only a little later but which in time seemed to lose all concern for real world issues.

Another exogenous change had a considerable impact on economics, but this time the impact was to make economics a more useful science. This was the development of the modern high-speed electronic computer. With this tool, and some improvements in the underlying econometric techniques, economists could begin to emulate more closely the work of natural scientists. While laboratory experiments in economics are generally precluded by the nature of the phenomena, an enhanced ability to measure events certainly improves economics' claim to scientific objectivity and methodology.

Nonetheless it is the discovery of new analytical models which may yet prove to have had the greatest impact on modern economics. Developments such as the theory of property rights, a greater understanding of the nature of the firm, rigorous analysis of public goods issues, theories of human capital, an appreciation of information and other transaction costs, rational expectations models, a theory of bureaucratic organizations, and the wealth of new ideas about pricing and other business practices have enriched the intellectual quality of economics enormously in the last twenty-five years.

But with all of this, economics remained largely academic and unrealistic until the full import of intermixing law and economics was understood. The 1920's had witnessed the development of a school known as "institutionalism." It never dominated economic thought because it tended to emphasize descriptions of real-world behavior almost to the exclusion of analytical theory. The modern field of law and economics, however, avoids this problem by adopting both the keen appreciation for details characteristic of law as well as the best of modern economic analysis.

The stage was now set, at least intellectually, for major advances in our ability to analyze policy issues and to prescribe policy. The circle was complete: law now had a scientific and objective analytical apparatus available to it, and economics could proceed with much less danger of being purely pedantic and irrelevant.

The marriage has already proved to be remarkably successful. Hardly a category of law has not been touched by this interdisciplinary breakthrough. Such disparate areas as personal injury law, discrimination, environmental regulation, antitrust, and domestic relations have fallen under the influence of "imperial economics." Economics is now taught in well over half of all fully accredited law schools in the United States, and there are between twelve and fifteen centers for research, teaching, publication, and conferences in law and economics. More dramatically, courses variously entitled "Law and Economics" are taught at over 450 colleges and universities in the United States. There are presently five journals of law and economics published in England and America, with at least three more announced for future publication. Law professors and judges queue up for years to attend intensive courses in microeconomic theory. Indeed they are cut off from a significant portion of modern scholarly writing without this training.

There are today hundreds of scholars professionally trained in law and economics, and the number is growing rapidly. And yet the ultimate impact of this intellectual revolution is not in sight.

One thing, however, does seem worth concluding about this development. As we have noted, the older mechanical approach to law, in an era of enormous social concerns, lent itself to easy moralizing and to the polemical zeal of reformers. Legal process, set loose from ancient moorings in tradition and precedent, but without an objective or scientific guideline, becomes arbitrary and can easily be turned against the cause of individual freedom. By the same token an economic science devoid of any inherent concern for individual rights and orderly procedures could also readily become a tool of totalitarianism, precisely as Marxian theorists urge on behalf of "scientific socialism."

But the two disciplines, each with its separate profound roots, one in science and one in dispute resolution, offer at least a fair chance that scholarship in the future may be increasingly used in the interest of human liberty and welfare. It is doubtful that Anglo-American law will ever return to anything like its natural law origins and its seemingly mechanical decision-making techniques. Nor is it likely that economics will ever return to the innocence which made it almost totally irrelevant to real world considerations. But it is likely that the integrated discipline of law and economics will continue to flourish and to aid in the search for the good society.

Chapter 9

The Tension of Order and Freedom in the University

RUSSELL KIRK

U niversities were founded to sustain faith by reason. My own university, St. Andrews, was established in the fifteenth century by the Scottish Inquisitor of Heretical Pravity, to resist the Lollards' errors. The early universities' teaching imparted both order and freedom to the intellect; and that was no paradox, for order and freedom exist necessarily in a healthy tension.

But in our day, as in various earlier times, many universities have lost any clear general understanding of either freedom or order, intellectually considered. So it seems worthwhile to review here the relationship between order and freedom, and the part of a university in maintaining the tension between the two.

Indulge me first in some observations concerning the connection between faith, order, and freedom, all of which are intertwined in university studies. In recent generations, a great many professors have failed to apprehend the connection. Let us commence with that popular but vague term "freedom."

Freedom is normal for mankind. I mean that ordered liberty is natural for truly human persons. Yet human freedom, like much else in human normality, is denied at least as often as it is affirmed.

The word "normal" does not really mean "average" or "generally accepted": it means "enduring standard." Human beings have the power either of observing the norms of their nature, or of violating them. So it is that the periods of true freedom in society, throughout the course of history, have been shorter than the periods of servitude. Under God, men and women have the privilege and the peril of choosing the life they will lead. Much of the time, in ages past and today, men have used their moral freedom to choose slavery or anarchy instead of ordered liberty.

Living as we Americans do in a nation still substantially free, and perhaps at the end of what has been called the "liberal era," many of us take for granted a degree of freedom which has been bestowed upon us by the painful labors and experiences of our ancestors, over many generations — and which may be ruined in the space of a few years by our folly or neglect. Freedom already has vanished from much of the modern world, and in many lands it never took root. Unless we understand the origins and ends of our liberty, we Americans may learn what it is to lose freedom in a fit of absence of mind. And if the nature of freedom is misunderstood in the universities, it will be misunderstood everywhere.

As I read history, it seems to me that a high degree of ordered, civilized freedom is linked closely to religious belief. Most liberals of the eighteenth and nineteenth centuries were willing enough to agree that there existed some connection between liberty and property. Yet many of those liberals ignored or denied the bond between religious faith and ordered freedom. "We learn from history that we learn nothing from history," Hegel wrote, in irony. If the great troubles of our time teach mankind anything, surely we ought now to recognize that true freedom cannot endure in a society which denies a transcendent order. A university which ridicules the claims of the transcendent must end without intellectual coherence — and without genuine intellectual freedom.

The first people to be freed from the spiritual servitude of the ancient empires were the Hebrews. It was consciousness of their duty and their hope as children of God that gave them resolution to withstand the life-in-death of the great nations which surrounded them.

A degree of personal freedom still higher was achieved by certain Greek peoples in the sixth and fifth centuries before Christ. This noble freedom decayed when the old Greek religion and morality gave way to sophistry, and "the rude son might strike the father dead." The genius of Socrates, Plato, and Aristotle did not suffice to restore the Greek freedom of spirit and law, once the belief in the divine ordering of things had dissolved.

Among the Romans, freedom endured so long as the high old Roman virtue flourished: so long as the Roman piety moved men, the disciplines of *labor, pietas, fatum.* Yet out of the ruins of Rome grew the highest order of liberty man has known: Christian freedom. The depressed masses of the proletariat were given hope by the word of Christ; the barbarians were taught restraint by the Word. Humanity learnt the lesson of the suffering servant.

Medieval liberties, in great part, were the product of Christian belief. The rights of the towns, the independence of the guilds, the code of chivalry — these arose out of faith in what Burke called "the contract of eternal society."

So modern freedom is not the creation of a few enthusiastic revolutionaries. Rather, it is a heritage laboriously developed in suffering. Freedom cannot endure unless we are willing to nurture the religious understanding that is its sanction; unless we maintain the springs of ordered liberty. It is worth remarking that the nineteenth-century ideology of "liberalism" generally ignored its religious sources. Some of those liberals, without understanding of the sources, thought of freedom as wholly secular and utilitarian, man-made. Others thought of freedom as a political abstraction, unrelated to religious concepts or to ancient usages. Both these "liberal" views have been hostile toward the Christian idea of the "person" under God. Such liberalism has dominated the university for a century and more — and not merely in state universities.

In the closing decades of the twentieth century, when most of the world is subject to arbitrary dominations, it is the urgent duty of the university to restore an apprehension of the sources of freedom. Even among a people who boast of their liberty, freedom may be lost at the moment of its seeming triumph. Stand upon the Acropolis of Athens, or on the Roman Capitoline, or on the Rock of Athena, at Agrigento, and look upon the ruins. The material splendor of those societies was at its height not long before the collapse of faith and liberty. In the name of democracy, of equality, of social justice, it is possible to overturn speedily the genuine order and justice and freedom of modern civilization. "And that house fell; and great was the fall of that house." The university — which Dante called one of the three powers governing society, along with church and state — can ignore the true character of freedom only at the university's grave peril. So let me turn to some brief observations on the relationship between freedom and order, considered intellectually and socially.

"Orders and degrees," John Milton says, "jar not with liberty, but well consist." I believe that we will be unable, in the university or out of it, to maintain any successful defense of our freedoms until we recognize afresh those principles of order under which freedom in our heritage acquired real meaning. Every right is married to a duty; every freedom owns a corresponding responsibility; and there cannot be genuine freedom unless there exists also genuine order, in the moral realm and in the social realm.

I am saying this: in any just society, there subsists a healthy tension between the claims of order and the claims of freedom: when that tension is well maintained, it is possible to obtain a large measure of justice. This clear understanding was the principal contribution of Edmund Burke to political theory; and the attempt to achieve such a tension or balance is the principal problem of modern practical politics.

Order, in the moral realm, is the realizing of a body of transcendent norms — indeed, a hierarchy of norms or standards — which give purpose to existence and motive to conduct. Order, in society, is the harmonious arrangement of classes and functions which guards justice and obtains willing consent to law and ensures that we all shall be safe together. Although there cannot be freedom without order, in some sense there occurs always a conflict between the claims of order and the claims of freedom. Often we express this conflict as the competition between the desire for liberty and the desire for security.

Modern technological developments and modern mass democracy have made this struggle more intense. President Washington observed that "individuals entering into a society must give up a share of their liberty to preserve the rest." Yet doctrinaires of one ideology or an other, in our time, continue to cry out for absolute security, absolute order; or for absolute freedom, power to assert the ego in defiance of all convention. During the past two decades, this clash was readily observed on the typical American campus. I suggest that in asserting freedom as an absolute, somehow divorced from order, we repudiate our heritage of freedom and expose ourselves to the peril of absolutism — whether that absolutism be what Tocqueville calls "democratic despotism" or what recently existed in Germany and now stands triumphant in Russia, China, and other countries. "To begin with unlimited freedom," Dostoevski wrote in *The Devils*, "is to end with unlimited despotism."

When some people — E. H. Carr in England, for instance, or David Lilienthal in America — talk of "freedom," they seem to mean, really, "material prosperity for the many." Now material prosperity, pure economic "security," is not the same thing as either freedom or order. Nor is it the same thing as happiness. An Athenian slave might be more comfortable than many a free man, but he was not free.

It is quite possible that the person who desires freedom and the benefits of order must be prepared to sacrifice a degree of security. A slave, in Aristotle's definition, is a being who allows others to make his choices for him. It is quite possible for a man to be materially prosperous, freed from the necessity of choice, and yet servile. It also is possible that such a man may suffer no outrageous oppression. But he must always lack one thing, this servile man, and that is true manhood, the dignity of man. He remains a child; he never comes into man's birthright, which is the pleasure and the pain of making one's own choices.

Some of these problems of freedom upon which I have touched glancingly are examined by John Stuart Mill in his essay *On Liberty* — a little treatise which has done much to confuse universities' discussion of freedom from his day until ours. There may be found value in that essay; but I think there also is weakness in it, and peril; and adulation of Mill tends to confuse serious examination of the difficulties of liberty in the year of Our Lord 1981. We live in the twentieth century, not the nineteenth, and we now experience distresses to which Mill never was exposed. Yet Professor Henry Steele Commager, not many years ago, informed us that "we cannot too often repair to John Stuart Mill's *On Liberty*," implying that this essay, like the laws of the Medes and the Persians, is immutable. Mill was unaware of any difficulty in closely defining "Liberty" — unlike Cicero, who saw the necessity for distinguishing between *libido* and *voluntas*. To Mill, "liberty" might mean "doing as one likes" or "pursuing one's own good in one's own way" or acting "according to one's own inclinations and judgment."

At present, Mill's arguments are being employed interestingly by persons who pretend to believe in an absolute freedom that no society ever has been able to maintain — and this in an age which requires the highest degree of cooperation, when "the great wheel of circulation" upon which our economy and our security depend necessarily is more to us than ever before. Such use of the writings of Mill — or those of a different sort of philosopher, Rousseau — may be encountered among enthusiasts of the New Left, and also among zealots of the "libertarian" Radical Right. Some of these persons — curiously archaic in their opinions, although they pride themselves upon their preoccupation with "relevance" — are oldfangled Benthamite liberals, dedicated to economic individualism in the age of the atomic pile; others (and these more ominous) are the newfangled collectivistic liberals, desirous of receiving everything from the state, but insistent that they owe nothing in return — not even loyalty.

So my general argument is this: liberty, prescriptive freedom as we Americans have known it, cannot endure without order. Our constitutions were established that order might make possible true freedom. Despite all our American talk of private judgment, dissent, and individualism, still our national character has the stamp of a respect for order almost superstitious in its power: respect for the moral order ordained by religion, and for the prescriptive political forms which we, more than any other people in this twentieth century, have maintained little altered. We would do immense mischief to our freedom if we ceased to respect our established order, running instead after an abstract, Jacobin liberty.

What is deficient in the thought of Mill and his disciples, it seems to me, is an adequate understanding of the principles of order. First, any coherent and beneficial freedom, surely, must have the sanction of moral order: it must refer to doctrines, religious in origin, that establish a hierarchy of values and set bounds to the ego. Second, any coherent and beneficial freedom must know the check of social order: it must accord with a rule of law, regular in its operation, that recognizes and enforces prescriptive rights, protects minorities against majorities and majorities against minorities, and gives meaning to the concept of human dignity.

Freedom as an abstraction is the liberty in whose name crimes are committed. But freedom, as realized in the separate, limited, balanced, well-defined rights of persons and groups, operating within a society moved by moral principles, is the quality which makes it possible for men and women to become truly human.

These things have been said often before. But every grand question has to be argued afresh in every generation, and especially in the universities. We need, I repeat, to refresh the understanding of "freedom" even among the learned, or perhaps especially among the learned.

For when many people, professors included, employ nowadays this word "freedom," they use it in the sense of the French Revolutionaries: freedom from tradition, freedom from established social institutions, freedom from religious doctrines, freedom from prescriptive duties. One thinks of Robert Louis Stevenson's little exercise in mockery, "The Four Reformers":

Four reformers met under a bramble bush. They were all agreed that the world must be changed. "We must abolish property," said one.

"We must abolish marriage," said the second.

"We must abolish God," said the third.

"I wish we could abolish work," said the fourth.

"Do not let us get beyond practical politics," said the first. "The first thing is to reduce men to a common level."

"The first thing," said the second, "is to give freedom to the sexes."

"The first thing," said the third, "is to find out how to do it."

"The first step," said the first, "is to abolish the Bible."

"The first thing," said the second, "is to abolish the laws."

"The first thing," said the third, "is to abolish mankind."

This mood is what Santayana mordantly called "freedom from the consequences of freedom," confounding nihilism with liberation. For we do not live in an age that is oppressed by the dead weight of archaic establishments and obsolete customs. The peril in our time, rather, is that the foundations of the great deep will be broken up, and that the swift pace of alteration will make it impossible for generation to link with generation. Our era, necessarily, should be what Matthew Arnold called an epoch of concentration. Or, at least, the thinking American, in the university as out of it, needs to turn his talents to concentration, the reconstruction of our moral and social heritage. This is an age not for anarchic freedom, but for ordered freedom.

There survive older and stronger concepts of freedom than that proclaimed by the French Jacobins; and more consistent concepts than that of Mill. In Christian teaching, freedom is submission to the will of God. This is no paradox. As he who would save his life must lose it, so the person who desires true freedom must recognize an order that gives all freedoms their sanction. This lacking, freedom becomes at best the liberty of those who possess power at the moment to do as they like with the lives of those whose interests conflict with theirs.

In the Christian understanding, as in the Judaic tradition and the Stoic philosophy and in Indic thought, there subsists also the conviction that freedom may be attained through abstinence. Not to lust after the things of the flesh, or after power, or after fame: this is true freedom, the freedom of Stilbo confronting the conqueror, or of Socrates before the Athenian jury. This is the freedom of Diogenes asking Alexander to stand out of the sun. The man who has made his peace with the universe is free, however poor he may be; the man bent upon gratifying his appetites is servile, however rich he may be. This freedom from desire, once taught within universities, has a strange ring in universities of our day.

Personal freedom must be found within a moral order. And public freedom must be found within a well-maintained social order; it must be the product of a common historical experience, of custom, of convention. We live in an age which, for good or ill, has come to depend upon the highest degree of cooperation and discipline ever known to civilization. Our economy, our very political structure, might not abide for twenty-four hours the triumph of that "absolute liberty" of the individual preached by Lamartine and other enthusiasts of the nineteenth century. As Simone Weil put it, "Order is the first need of all."

Within today's university, collectivistic prejudices and libertarian prejudices frequently coexist within the same professor, insane conjunction. Both collectivism and libertarianism are the enemies of ordered freedom. Various of my colleagues at this retreat have dealt hard knocks to collectivism; so, time considered, let me cudgel today's libertarianism as inimical to freedom.

Once upon a time, the university maintained authority; indeed, the university *was* authority. But today a great many people within the Academy will submit to no authority, temporal or spiritual. They desire to be different, in morals as in politics. In our highly tolerant society, such extreme individualism seems an amusing pose. Its consequences may become unamusing.

Thus the professorial libertarian of our day delights in eccentricity. Did not John Stuart Mill himself commend eccentricity as a defense against deadening democratic conformity? He rejoices, today's libertarian, in strutting political eccentricity, as in strutting moral eccentricity. But, as James Fitzjames Stephen commented on Mill, "Eccentricity is far more often a mark of weakness than a mark of strength. Weakness wishes, as a rule, to attract attention by trifling distinctions, and strength wishes to avoid it."

Amen to that. I have quoted Stevenson; let me turn now to G. K. Chesterton on eccentricity and anarchic liberty. Gabriel Gale, the intuitive hero of Chesterton's collection of stories entitled *The Poet and the Lunatics*, speaks up for centricity: "Genius oughtn't to be eccentric! It ought to be the core of the cosmos, not on the revolving edges. People seem to think it a compliment to accuse one of being an outsider, and to talk about the eccentricities of genius. What would they think if I

127

said I only wish to God I had the centricities of genius?"

The academic libertarians' dream of an absolute private freedom is one of those visions that issue from between the gates of ivory; and the dreadful speed with which society moves today flings the libertarians outward through centrifugal force, even to the outer darkness, where there is wailing and gnashing of teeth. The final emancipation from religion, convention, custom, and order is annihilation — "whirled/Beyond the circuit of the shuddering Bear/In fractured atoms."

In his little-known book entitled *The Poet and the Lunatics*, Chesterton offers us a parable of such licentious freedom: a story called "The Yellow Bird". To an English country house comes Professor Ivanhov, a Russian scholar who has published *The Psychology of Liberty*. He is a zealot for emancipation, expansion, the elimination of limits. Ivanhov begins by liberating a canary from its cage — to be torn to pieces in the forest. He proceeds to liberate the goldfish by smashing their bowl. He ends by blowing up himself and the beautiful old house where he has been a guest.

"What exactly is liberty?" inquires a spectator of this series of events — Gabriel Gale, Chesterton's mouthpiece. "First and foremost, surely, it is the power of a thing to be itself. In some ways the yellow bird was free in the cage. It was free to be alone. It was free to sing. In the forest its feathers would be torn to pieces and its voice choked forever. Then I began to think that being oneself, which is liberty, is itself limitation. We are limited by our brains and bodies; and if we break out, we cease to be ourselves, and, perhaps, to be anything."

The Russian psychologist could not endure the necessary conditions of human existence; he must eliminate all limits; he could not endure the "round prison" of the overarching sky. But his alternative was annihilation for himself and his lodging; and he took that alternative. He ceased to be anything but fractured atoms. That is the ultimate freedom of the frantic libertarian. If, *per imposible*, American society should accept the leadership of libertarian ideologues — why, this Republic might end in fractured atoms, with a Russian touch to the business.

Against license, anarchy, and chaos, the university was raised up, to restrain passion and prejudice through right reason. What the university offers to intellects is discipline and order.

Through such intellectual order and discipline, rational liberty of the person and of the society is made possible. This is true of the humane and the social studies; it is quite as true of the physical sciences. The university is one important human response to the universal menace of chaos. I think of some sentences written by an English biologist, Lyall Watson.

"Chaos is coming," Dr. Watson reminds us. "It is written in the laws of thermodynamics. Left to itself, everything tends to become more and more disorderly until the final and natural state of things is a completely random distribution of matter. Any kind of order, even that as simple as the arrangement of atoms in a molecule, is unnatural and happens only by chance encounters that reverse the general trend. These events are statistically unlikely, and the further combination of molecules into anything as highly organized as a living organism is wildly improbable. Life is a rare and unreasonable thing.

"The continuance of life depends on the maintenance of an unstable situation. It is like a vehicle that can be kept on the road only by continual running repairs and by access to an endless supply of spare parts. Life draws its components from the environment. From the vast mass of chaotic probability flowing by, it extracts only the distinctive improbabilities, the little bits of order among the general confusion. Some of those it uses as a source of energy, which it obtains by the destructive process of digestion; from others, it gets the information it needs to ensure continued survival. This is the hardest part, extracting order from disorder, distinguishing those aspects of the environment that carry useful information from those which simply contribute to the over-all process of decay. Life manages to do this by a splendid sense of the incongruous." So Watson puts the truth in his chapter entitled "Cosmic Law and Order."

The university is meant to assist in life's struggle for survival, by extracting order from disorder. Studies in seventeenth-century literature and ancient history and quantum mechanics all are paths to order. And also they are paths to freedom; for the unexamined life is a servile life, not worth living. The university is not intended to be a staging-ground for the destruction of order in personality and order in society; on the contrary, the university's mission (to paraphrase John Henry Newman) is to impart a philosophical habit of mind.

Men and women of a philosophical habit of mind are free intellectually. If their influence upon a society is strong, that society is free politically. Such private and public freedom is made possible by the ordering of mind and conscience. For the university, as for society generally, freedom and order are ends of equal importance, existing at once in symbiosis and in tension. So it is that when a university forgets the ordering and integrating of knowledge, it impairs the freedom of the mind. And then chaos rushes upon us.